To Marilyn, Kelly, Greg

and Quilly

Published under license from Stargate Educational Services by
Heartbeat Productions Inc.
Box 633
Abbotsford, BC V2T 6Z8
email: info@heartbeat1.com

Second Edition

Copyright © 2016 by Paul A. Lamarre, Ph.D. All rights reserved,
No part of this information may be reproduced, modified, or redistributed without
the prior written permission of the publisher, author or copyright holder.

Designed by Victory Design Associates

Published in Canada

E-Version ISBN   978-1-895112-50-4
Print ISBN   978-1-895112-51-1

The software text and images are owned and copyrighted by Paul A. Lamarre and/or Stargate Educational Services and are protected by Canadian and International copyright law, as well as international trade provisions on all formats.

Overview

Preparation for learning to read is far more efficient and cost-effective than remediation. After more than 20 years of teaching beginning Grade One students who can barely recite the alphabet, three things are very clear. First, parents play a vital role in the preparation for Grade One while their children are in Kindergarten. Second, there is a strong need for a low cost program that parents can use, at home, in a time-frame of half an hour or less. Third, it is essential that the materials develop skills that meet the teacher's expectations of what the children can say and do when they enter the Grade One classroom.

Several key factors contribute to becoming a good, proficient reader:

- The child has to know the basic elements of the reading code. Children who are sent on to Grade One able to recite the alphabet are at an advantage. If they can recognize and name the individual letters accurately, they are even better prepared to learn to read.
- The good reader is one who instantly recognizes words. Once a word has been figured out through "sounding it out" or by other means, it must be committed to memory. Memory has to be trained and developed; it cannot be taken for granted.
- Students have to learn how to think, academically. They have to be taught how to process information they see and hear. They have to learn how to store sequences of information and to refer back to that information when asked a question to be able to provide the correct information. That requires specific training that is systematic.
- Students have to learn new concepts that teachers use when they give instructions. While the children may use those same concepts in their daily speaking patterns, parents and teachers have to make sure that they really know what the words mean.
- Finally, students have to develop the capacity to keep up with the teacher's pace of instruction. If "Janie" is always two or three paces behind the others in the class, she's going to have a difficult time keeping up. That may lead to frustration and discouragement.

What Alphabet Knowledge Means

Research tells us consistently that knowledge of the alphabet is the single, best predictor of academic success. Year after year, research studies confirm that what happens in the first few years shapes the child's academic and social well-being later in life. Children considered prepared to learn by the time they start Grade One are usually set for a life-time of academic success. Careful preparation and development of the skills needed is more efficient than remediation. Such preparation for learning is the driving force behind **Annie Ape - The Magic Bullet to Literacy.** It is designed to help parents discover and understand what alphabet knowledge means and why it is so important for their Kindergarten children.

A Comprehensive Program

Annie Ape - The Magic Bullet to Literacy is a powerful and comprehensive, alternate program. It establishes a climate for learning to read similar to the one in which the child learns to speak. Parents don't present formal speaking lessons to their infants and toddlers. Yet the child learns to speak in imitation to the speech that surrounds him. In the same way, and as much as possible, **Annie** presents the skills needed to learn to read in a natural environment so that learning to read can take place. It is such an understandable and comprehensive process that some children seem to be able to read spontaneously toward the end of the program. Others go on to learn to read in the classroom, seemingly with little effort. **Annie Ape** prepares the child so that reading can take place, naturally, when the child feels the need.

Who Can Use the Material

The activities in **Annie Ape - The Magic Bullet to Literacy** are those that most parents WOULD DO, if only THEY KNEW. **Annie Ape** was designed to help parents discover what constitutes knowledge of the alphabet, how to determine readiness for learning, and to help them attain that goal. There are no pre-requisite skills beyond a commitment of time from the parent to the child.

Read through the overview from beginning to end, at least once. It is good to have a general idea of what information is going to be presented and how best to use it. The overview is important. If it appears a bit overwhelming, at first, it will sort itself out as the strategy is put to use. After a while, it will flow logically and efficiently. Don't be surprised if you discover additional ideas for use of the material.

Annie supports any and all Kindergarten programs.

Time Commitment

Annie Ape asks for a commitment of time from the parent to the child. The commitment is a daily 20-30 minute period, for 90 days. The outcome of those 45 hours is a greater knowledge and understanding of the child's learning strengths.

Follow the suggestions given in this manual, spending no more than 20 to 30 minutes a day. There are no formalized reading lessons to present. The question strategy that you need to develop the knowledge required for proficient reading is prepared for you.

Your teaching skill is confirmed. You have taught your child many things. Your teaching doesn't stop because the child goes to school. Your expertise doesn't vanish simply because your child is in school. Most importantly, working with your child reinforces the concept that learning to read is important. Instead of reading stories, you will be reading questions and judging the accuracy of the answers. That is the only difference.

About the Materials

The basic package components are highly useful and flexible. There is no need to go out and purchase more and more expensive single-purpose material.

The alphabet cards contained in the manual are presented in lower case letters. To help in teaching printing, the arrows show how to form the letters.

Colorful and clear, there is a different picture plate for each letter of the alphabet. The letter story at the bottom of each plate is used to reinforce letter naming, to identify individual words, to present ordinal understanding and to increase comprehension. The imagery is useful for the development of visual literacy, language and concept development. Since there are numerous objects on each card, counting and estimating become part of the program, as well.

The four-line printing sheets show how letters are positioned on the lines when they appear in words. High letters, low letters, and middle letters can be seen clearly.

The concepts that are presented for development are those that are used in giving instructions to Kindergarten to Grade 3 students. Often, these same words are used by the children in their day to day speech but are not really understood. Children who really understand these concepts usually perform very well in school.

The lesson procedure and question strategy for each letter story are included at the end of this overview.

Overview

The overview is intended to identify the components of a good preparation for learning in Kindergarten/Grade One. It will highlight the importance of including each particular component. Why is it important? What is the goal? What will this do for the learner?

Letter Name Recognition

The child has to be able to recite the alphabet by rote. A way to gain efficiency is to have the child look at the letters, while saying them, so that later, when a letter is presented it will be correctly identified by name.

In order to reduce confusion, always keep the letters in alphabetical order. If the letters are presented in random order before the child has a firm grasp of the names of the letters, confusion will result in guessing. Once the guessing pattern is established, it is very, very difficult to extinguish.

Every session should begin with a review of the alphabet. It is simply impossible to overlearn the alphabet. Saying the alphabet together with the child, as the cards are presented, helps the child see it, say it, and hear it, to help establish mastery. Do this for several weeks on a daily basis. It is useful to review it on a weekly basis once mastery is clearly established.

Continual review sets the child up for success. It also provides the necessary repetition that, in turn, reduces the response time. The child who has instant recognition and instant response time is at a distinct advantage for reading instruction.

Letter Name Recognition, Part 2

At the point where you sense that the child can name the letters correctly at about the 95 percent level of accuracy, or higher, it is time to present the letters in reverse order, that is, from Z to A. This exercise will take the task beyond rote memory into clear recognition of the letter. This exercise proves whether the child knows the names of the letters, or not.

Once again, to set the child up for success, always begin this exercise by reciting the names of the letters with the child as they are presented from Z to A. Depending on the progress of the child, it may be necessary to repeat this step for several days, or even weeks, before asking the child to do it on his or her own. If the process is rushed, the child will feel the pressure and will begin to guess. It is better to avoid spending time correcting errors and working to get rid of the habit of guessing.

Randomization

When reverse order (Z to A) checkouts reach the 95 percent, or higher, level of accuracy, it is time to randomize the letters. Rather than do it artificially, the best and most realistic source to find the random presentation of letters is in any print source: book, magazine, newspaper, cereal box...anything that has print on it. Ask the child to focus on a line of print and say the names of the letters in the order of appearance.

If the source is appropriate to the child, after the letter identification, read the sentence aloud. It will demonstrate that the letters come together to form words and ideas, which is the ultimate purpose of doing the preparatory work. Reading the sentence aloud provides closure to the activity. As well, it stimulates information processing and thinking.

It will also stimulate holding a system in mind while searching for the information. In other words, the child has to hold the alphabet in mind, look at a letter, and identify it correctly. Continued practice will stimulate improved speed of recognition of letters by name, accurately. Reading the sentence demonstrates the communication of an idea. If the sentence runs on to the next line, it presents an opportunity to demonstrate the purpose of an end mark.

Word Boundaries

We cannot expect that, because we know what a word is, the beginning learner will know that, too. We have to teach the child that the white spaces between words let us know where one word ends and another begins. The white spaces carry meaningful information. Without the white spaces, it is much more difficult to read.

How can we expect a child who doesn't know the alphabet or recognize the letters by name to know what a word is. We can't! We have to teach it.

Primary teachers usually refer to word boundaries in the students' printing work as "finger spacing." Every child needs to understand in reading and in writing that the spaces between the words signify the boundaries of words.

Word Recognition and Word Identification

Once a letter story is introduced, it provides another series of randomized letters that may be used for drill in letter name recognition. Each letter story has four words with three word boundaries. So, when the child is asked to show or point to a specific word in the letter story, she has the background to be able to figure out which word it is in the sequence. The concept of word is reinforced. The concept of word boundary is reinforced. The development of memory is reinforced. And, when all of the information is brought together to provide the right answer, that mental activity is called ***thinking***.

At this level, the thinking is quite visible. The child vocalizes the story to be able to identify the word requested. That done, the child is then asked to spell the word, which reinforces letter-name recognition. After the word is spelled, the child is asked to tell you what word was spelled. Then the child is asked to recite the letter story again to reinforce memory for words and to prepare for comprehension.

Comprehension

The purpose of writing is to communicate ideas. The purpose in reading is to receive and understand the ideas communicated in writing.

Each of the letter stories in **Annie Ape** is a complete sentence. Simple comprehension questions from the storyline are basic. They set the stage for understanding in later grades. Asking the basic "W" questions begins the formation of habits that we need to develop to become good readers: Who? What? Where? When? Why?

Language Acquisition

Every primary child is in the process of developing language skills. The imagery in **Annie Ape** is very useful toward that end. A good question strategy will enrich the child's receptive and expressive language. Does the child understand the words that people use? How varied is the language that he uses to express himself?

The purpose behind the imagery is for the child to talk...to develop precision and clarity of expression. Discussions about the pictures and the fantasy or reality of the letter stories contribute to the development of good language skills in the child. Color, the quality of the illustrations, names, placement of objects are all potent sources of questions to stimulate thinking, understanding and language usage. Good use of language is a powerful source of grammatical information from which the child generates the rules and patterns of our language.

The stories in **Annie Ape - the Magic Bullet to Literacy** have a strong syllabic beat. The stories are easy to remember because of it.

It is important to understand that children need time to process the information of the question and then to do a search of stored information and prepare the answer. That takes time. Often, if it takes more than 2-3 seconds for the child to answer, adults unwittingly begin to fill the silence. The child, of course, may feel thwarted and may conclude that the answer is not important. If that becomes a habit, "yes/no" questions become the standard. In new and unfamiliar territory, it takes time to conduct the brain search for the information requested.

If the adult does all the talking, the child simply cannot develop expressive language skills.

Spelling

There is a strong relationship between the ability to identify and name letters correctly and accurate spelling. Timely recognition of letters also affects speed of decoding and effective oral reading. Seeing and naming all the letters in a word reduces guessing based on the first letter or first few letters.

The tendency to guess at words develops frequently and with intensity in those students who have difficulty with phonics and blending. When the child knows the alphabet and when the child can identify each letter, accurately, by name, it is appropriate to incorporate spelling in each lesson. Any time a word is taken out of context for spelling, it should not be left in its segmented form, that is, s-p-e-l-l.

Asking the child to tell you the word spelled represents closure of the word. Closure also helps the child relate the word to his or her listening and speaking vocabularies.

Ordinals

When the child can point to any word with ease, it is time to introduce ordinals. First, second, third, fourth, then, next, after, and last are ordinal concepts with frequent use in instructional language. Because of it, it is useful to children to have at least a basic understanding of most of these concepts in Kindergarten. Understanding ordinals is crucial to future success in school.

Assignments follow an ordinal sequence of events. Problem-solving strategies imply ordinals. Ordinals affect outcomes outside the school experience: Cooking, carpentry, sewing, car maintenance and repair.

Colors

The illustrations in **Annie Ape** are intentionally colorful. Experiment with the primary colors to make the secondary colors. Make many references to color as you work through the alphabet.

Concepts

The concepts incorporated into the picture plates are those usually found in primary instructional materials. Although the child may use these concepts is everyday speech, there is no guarantee that the child understands the concepts he or she uses.

For concepts to be understood, they must be presented in pairs…as opposites: front/back; in/out. In order to understand what front is, I must know what back is. They go together.

For that reason, only introduce one pair at a time. Work that one set to a level of comfort in function before introducing another set. If introduced too quickly, confusion will set in. Maintain a good review schedule for those introduced earlier.

The lesson section has a fairly extensive list of questions covering many concepts. Pick and choose the questions that relate specifically to the concepts being taught and reinforced. Work at developing a good level of understanding with the concepts. The child who enters grade one with a good sense of concept is set up for success.

Counting

There is ample material in the illustrations to develop familiarity with counting, number concept, and estimating. There are images in the letter, out of the letter, at the top, at the bottom, to the left, to the right, and in the corners. All can be used for counting; some can be used for estimating.

How many bowls of noodles are in the letter 'n?' If the child responds, "One hundred," that would be clear evidence that the child's concept of number is very superficial.

Memory

Memory is assumed to be present in all children. It is rarely, if ever, taught as a specific skill. The importance of memory in reading cannot be overstated. The more quickly a word is recognized, the more easily it is logged and understood.

Annie Ape teaches visual, sequential memory. The child can recite all letter stories by looking at the picture plates. The child can recite all the letter stories by looking at the letter cards.

Annie Ape teaches auditory, sequential memory the child can recite all letter stories by hearing the name of the letter. The child can recite all letter stories by hearing the sound of the first letter in the story.

The final test for memory requires the child to recite all letter stories with no visual or auditory cues. The child recites 26 letter stories — 104 words — in proper sequence.

If the child gets "stuck," see it as confusion in information processing, as the need for more practice in the skill, or as the need for a problem-solving strategy. Extend to the child the courtesy of asking for help, if needed, and the kind of help appropriate to the situation. It could mean a request to look at the picture plate, the letter card, the initial sound, asking for the name of the animal or the kind of animal to trigger the recall. At times, several sounds may be needed. The child will always request help in the preferred mode of learning.

Articulation in Speech

It is important to have the child articulate as clearly as possible when reciting the letter stories. Many children love to say them as fast as they can. In doing so, they often misarticulate. The request for clear articulation allows for the identification of speech difficulties, which can be corrected in a non-threatening manner, over time.

Text Properties

Children do not always see or understand proportion in the terms we use. Why is it that we expect children to see what we see, when we have clear evidence that they do not? If we look at the printed alphabet, we see that there are high letters (ascending letters), middle letters, and low letters (descending letters), as in **bag**.

The four-line Letter-Trace pages provided for you will help the children make the transition to traditionally lined paper if worked carefully and diligently. Check with the local teachers' store to see if scribblers of this type are available in your area.

The letter cards for alphabet drill have arrows showing proper letter formation. Use of this approach will make handwriting easier when it is introduced in Grade Three.

Letter Formation

Prominence in **Annie Ape** is given to lower case letters. Why? On average, 95 percent of what is read is printed in lower case letters. So, teach your child to print his or her name using lower case letters. And use the terminology upper case and lower case instead of big letters and little letters.

Phonemic Awareness

Phonemic awareness is a significant activity in most kindergarten classrooms in North America. Often it is a separate program. Phonemic awareness simply means that the child has some understanding of the sounds that are put together to form the words we use in the communication of ideas. It means hearing the sounds at the beginning of words, at the ending of words, and those that come in between.

Phonemic awareness is incorporated into the lesson structure of **Annie Ape**. Once a few letter stories are memorized, visual, auditory and phonemic memory sequences are integrated into the memory review structure of the lessons. **Annie Ape** establishes a coherent point of reference for the sound structure of our language that is easy to remember and easy to use.

Visual Literacy

Visual literacy is the ability to read pictures and illustrations and to extract information from them. Many of the lesson components contribute in a meaningful way toward visual literacy. Most children have to be taught to see and to read illustrations.

Physical Activity and Learning

There is a growing body of research that suggests a strong relationship between physical development and success in school. The strategies that children learn when they explore in supervised, risk-safe activities on the playground, in the gym, and in team sports can also be used in the classroom. Being able to do a cartwheel on the playground does not turn Johnny and Mary into good readers. However, children are actively engaged in learning when they are at play.

Neural networks that develop in the brain because of physical activity CAN also be used for intellectual activity. Scientists have found that a brain area known to facilitate muscle control also fosters memory for ordering information.

Conclusion

If you will do these activities, spending no more than 30 minutes a day, for 90 days, you will establish the readiness skills that are needed for successful entry to Grade One. These are the building blocks to self-directed, sustained attention. These are the building blocks to reading, spatial orientation, reasoning, and math.

At the end of this do not be surprised if your son or daughter "gets it" and learns to read. You will not have taught reading in any formal way. You will have established a natural environment so that learning to read can take place. It is a setting comparable to learning to speak.

You do not provide speaking lessons for your children. You simply provide the speech community from which the child learns to speak.

If you commit to this program with your child for 90 days and follow the suggested **lesson plan**, your child will be prepared for Grade One. You will know how your child learns best, whether by seeing or by hearing. You will know your child's learning strengths. You will be able to give specific examples.

You may also discover that your child has some learning problems. In that case, you will understand what they are and will be able to note areas of strength and areas of weakness when discussing your child with the teacher. You will be able to explain them to the teacher in specific terms. You will develop the courage to continue to work with your child because you discovered the need and you won't doubt it.

Activities to enhance physical development

Because of the strong correlation that physical activity has in intellectual activity, parents are encouraged to make contributions to physical development through their own initiative or through organized, community sports. The variety of organized activities in most communities is extensive.

- Teach your child to hippety hop, to hop on one foot, to hop with both feet, to hop in regular and irregular patterns (R,R,L or L,L,R).
- Play on the school jungle gym.
- Create obstacle courses, at home, out of boxes, pillows, cushions, or chairs.
- Play follow the leader while dancing like a ballerina, waddling like a duck, and moving like a skater or a skier.
- Teach your child to play kick the can, to walk on stilts, to play hopscotch, to play shadow tag on a sunny day.
- Register them in swimming lessons, karate, Tae Kwon Do, T-ball, soccer, gymnastics, skating or dancing.
- Set up a pendulum in the back yard, in a playroom, in a carport or garage. Allow a few weeks of free exploration. Then use the pendulum to develop balance and fine-motor coordination. Stand on one foot and kick the pendulum with the big toe, with the inside of the foot, with the outside of the foot, with the shin, with the knee, with the hip, with the tummy, with the chest, with the shoulder. Do the same activities standing on the other foot. Hit the ball with the chin, with the left cheek, with the right cheek, and with the forehead.
- Adjust the pendulum to a comfortable level in line with the elbows bent at 90 degrees. Hit the ball with alternating fingers: index, index; middle, middle; ring, ring; pinkie, pinkie; thumb, thumb. Reverse the procedure to complete the set.

When teaching something new, avoid long explanations and continued trial and error. Demonstrate how to do it asking the child to watch. Let the child do what he or she can remember. Then demonstrate again with the child watching. Let the child do what he or she can remember. If it is not done right, set the activity aside for another day.

Avoid the power struggle. Especially, do not push the child out of the way and explain again and again how to do it.

Take up the activity again the next day. Repeat the demonstration procedure twice, allowing the child to do what he or she can remember. Once the child finds the solution, the concept will be remembered. And if it has to be figured out repeatedly, that is part of learning. No-one learned to drive in one easy lesson!

This method provides the opportunity for thinking. It is an effective learning strategy.

Walking heel, toe along a clear line can improve balance. Standing on a balance board can improve balance. Standing on one foot and doing pendulum activities with the other foot can improve balance. When balance is improved, academic performance has a chance of improvement.

Language Arts Activities

Discuss the words of the stories and their meanings. Discuss your child's experiences with the animals and the concepts of the letter stories. Discuss the truth of the stories. Where do apes live? Are there ants in the jungle? Does an ape really eat ants? How?

Make other sentences using the animal in the story, or another animal beginning with the same letter. Annie Aardvark ate ants. Annie Ape ate apricots. Alice Ant ate artichokes.

Look through old magazines and catalogues to find pictures to cut and paste into a pictionary of your child's current and expanded vocabulary. If you, or your child, has artistic talent, illustrate the vocabulary. You may have to look in a dictionary, encyclopedia, or other reference material to find illustrations to copy. If you have a computer, use the clip art. There are many programs available. Work with your child in the selection process. You will be in another potent language development setting. Often there are many illustrations from which to select. If that is the case, you will be extending the visual literacy of the child while working on language development. Font style and size can factor into the finished product to be printed off.

Original works such as these take time. However, over time, they become family treasures that can be passed on to your grandchildren. They become potent sources of motivation for your grandchildren to learn to read.

Go to the public library. Get books of nursery rhymes. There are many. Read them. Discuss them. Memorize favorites. When discussing, let the child speak. Avoid asking yes/no questions. Ask your child what the illustrated nursery rhyme might look like. Let the child draw it for you.

While at the library, get other alphabet books. Talk about them. Compare them. Discuss the quality of the illustrations. Notice the detail. Which one does your child prefer? Why? What makes one more appealing than another? Make your time with the alphabet fun and effortless learning.

Read to your children every day. It is the best way to demonstrate that reading and learning are important. Read from any source. Explore trade books that deal with science and other subjects. They are found in the children's section of the library. It is good to read beyond fairy tales and picture books to children. What are your child's interests? Foster it through books. What is in the family gene pool? Foster it through books.

Let your children see you reading every day. Encourage your children to read every day.

Use Words that Encourage

Use phrases like: Good thinking, good printing, good listening, good remembering, and good seeing. These words will foster more of the same. They are encouraging. Encouraging words give heart to keep at it.

If they do not "get it," simply say, "We'll do it again, tomorrow." Use, "Give it a shot!" instead of "Do the best you can!" The former encourages effort; the latter begets whining if the child cannot do it, or do it well. Appreciate that performance levels vary from day to day.

Realize, also, that use of the phrases, "Good boy" and "Good girl" when the child does something right may lead to the conclusion of being bad in their absence.

Let's Get Started

You are now equipped with a great deal of information on what to do and why you need to do it. Each of the first few lessons will undoubtedly take a few days to complete. That's perfectly OK. Both you and your child need to become comfortable with the processes and expectations. Skip the parts of any lesson that require proficiency until that knowledge has been developed. Just remember to apply the skipped parts at a later date.

Many of the ideas you read in the overview have been incorporated into the question strategy of the early lessons. The lesson strategy for Annie Ape ate ants is four pages; Harley Hamster hates hawks has two pages.

You will become very proficient over time. You and your child are embarking on an educational adventure. If you stay the course and enjoy the trip, the goal will be all the more meaningful. As Henry Wadsworth Longfellow has said,

"Perseverance is a great element of success. If you only knock long enough and loud enough at the gate, you are sure to wake up somebody."

Note:

If you have selected the Black & White Picture Book to accompany the Question Strategy Manual, you will need to adjust the questions that relate to color in the lesson strategy to fit the palette you have selected.

Question Strategy

Annie Ape ate ants

Drill alphabet.

Even if your child can recite the alphabet by rote, it is important to present the alphabet cards in sequence to develop letter name recognition. Since it is impossible to overlearn the alphabet, this drill forms part of every lesson. If your child is in the initial stages of learning the alphabet, more repetitions are needed at the beginning of each lesson than if your child already has a grasp of letter name recognition. Please note that it is important to offer at least one visual presentation before asking for checkouts, be it rote recitation or letter name recognition.

A-Z

When you are reasonably sure that your child can recite the alphabet with 90 percent accuracy, present the cards (in alphabetical order) asking your child to name each letter as it appears. This is an alphabetical order checkout.

Z-A

When you are reasonably sure that your child can recognize and name the letters of the alphabet with 90 percent accuracy, or better, present the cards in reverse order (Z to A) asking your child to name each letter as it appears. This is a reverse order checkout.

Random Presentation for Developing Proficiency in Letter Name Recognition

When you are sure that your child has a firm grasp of letter name recognition through a 100 percent level of accuracy in reverse order checkout, it is time to introduce randomization in a realistic context.

Take any source of print...book, magazine, newspaper, cereal box....any source of print.

Open at any point. Have your child tell you the names of the letters for each word in a sentence or more. When your child has completed the exercise satisfactorily, read the sentence or sentences used. This will communicate the idea that letters are put together in words to form sentences or ideas.

Please note that speed and accuracy are the desirable goals. The faster, more accurate the processing, the better off the student will be in reading instruction.

Introduce Letter Story

Introduce Annie Ape ate ants. Drill it until your child can recite it on his/her own. You may drill it orally first and then show the picture or you may show the picture and drill it at the same time. Do what you think is most effective for your child.

Language development and Visual Literacy

Check out your child's understanding of the meanings of the words. Check out your child's personal experience with apes.

- What does an ape look like?
- Where have you seen one?
- Have you seen a real ape?
- Where?
- Who were you with?
- Why were you there?
- Was it a special day?
- What made the day special?
- Looking at the picture plate for Annie Ape ate ants, many, many questions spring to mind.
- Ask your child to define a sandwich. What is a sandwich? (A sandwich is some type of filling between two slices of bread.)
- What is Annie doing? (She's sitting on an anthill. She's getting ready to eat an antwich sandwich. She's looking at the antwich. She's holding the antwich in her hands. She's holding her hands up. She's resting her feet on the anthill. She's not paying attention to the coming and going of the ants.)
- What is Annie wearing?
- What is an anthill?
- What are the ants doing? (They are going in and out of the anthill. They are carrying food to the anthill. They are carrying apples to the anthill.)
- How are the ants carrying the apples? (On their backs.)
- Can ants really do that?

Color

Our vision allows us to see color. If your child is familiar with the basic colors, the picture plates are useful for review. If not, this is a good source of teaching material. Although color is incorporated into every lesson outline, it can be omitted or included, as the need arises and time allows. Proficiency in color naming is a readiness goal.

What are the terms we use to identify and describe color? The picture plate for Annie Ape ate ants includes red, blue, pink, brown, yellow, black, green, and white. Ask appropriate questions using color as a key factor.

- Show me a red apple.
- Show me a yellow apple.
- Show me a pink apron.
- Show me a blue shoe.
- Show me a black ant.
- Show me a brown ape.
- Show me a leaf. What color is it?
- Show me the inside of the apple. What color is it?

Comprehension

- What is the animal's name?
- What kind of animal is Annie?
- What did Annie do?
- What did the ape eat?
- Who ate ants?

Word Identification and Word Boundaries

Before you can expect your child to identify each of the words in the letter stories, you will have to teach your child about word boundaries. Simply stated, word boundaries are the white spaces between words. These spaces carry meaning since they tell us where one word ends and another begins.

- Show your child a picture plate.
- Show the space. Call them word boundaries.
- Ask how many there are?
- Point to them and count them. There are three.
- Let's count them together.
- What do we call the white spaces between words?
- Word boundaries!
- Good remembering!

Once the concept of word boundary is clearly established, say,

- Point to Annie.
- Point to Ape.
- Point to ate.
- Point to ants.

Point to...show me...which word is...are variations that can be used once the idea of word identification is clear to your child.

Spelling

If your child is proficient in identifying and naming the letters (Z-A), it is appropriate to ask that any word identified in the previous segment, be spelled.

- Show me apples.
- What word is it? (apples)
- Spell apples. (a-p-p-l-e-s)
- What word did you spell? (apples)

Asking for the word identified to be spelled helps focus attention on the elements of the word. This will have an impact on accurate spelling in writing. In fact, it is a tactic used by teachers to reinforce spelling. It is habit forming.

Ordinals

Most Kindergarten and first grade children have difficulty with ordinals as an idea. As the word implies, ordinal means the order in which the words appear. Ordinals have to be introduced very carefully and have to be taught and reviewed on many successive days. A short interval of a weekend can result in having to re-teach the concept. If your child is gaining initial exposure to the alphabet, leave out working with ordinals until he or she is comfortable with many of the other lesson processes before introducing them. (Ordinals are included in each lesson because of individual variation.) If and when you tackle ordinals, this is how you might approach them.

Ask how many words are in the story. There are four.
- Annie is word number one.
- Ape is word number two.
- Ate is word number three.
- Ants is word number four.
- Point to each word while saying one, two, three, four.

Do this several times.

Verify understanding.
- Which is word number one? Two? Three? Four?
- Watch and listen again. One, two, three, four, while pointing to each word.
- After three or four repetitions, switch to first, second, third, fourth.

Repeat that several times.

Children often recite along with you when they catch on to what is being introduced.

(Repeat this pattern with several letter stories before asking your child for the ordinals of the story. Moving too quickly can create confusion. Confusion and befuddlement are more difficult to clear up in terms of time and effort than the time it takes to establish a firm foundation of knowledge before checking for mastery. It is counterproductive to move too quickly. Please resist the temptation to forge ahead. This is a cumulative process. Your child needs to be comfortable in working through the information, the manner of presentation, and what is expected before being asked to ingest new information on a daily basis.)

Concepts

Concepts are part of language development but they form a distinct category of ideas. The child needs careful introduction to the words used in establishing his or her position in space or the relationship of the child to the outside world. How does the child relate in time? How does the child relate to the printed page?

Pairs of concepts that might be explored are: On/off; to/from; in/out; coming/going; left/right; large/small; and whole/part.
- How are the ants carrying the apples? (On their backs.)
- Show me an ant carrying a whole apple.
- Show me an ant carrying part of an apple.
- Show me an ant carrying an apple core.
- Point to the ants that are coming to the anthill.
- Point to the ants that are going from the anthill.
- Point to an ant that is on the letter **a**.
- Point to an ant that is off the letter **a**.
- Show me an ant that is going in to the anthill.
- Show me an ant that is coming out of the anthill.
- Point to a large apple.
- Point to a small apple.
- Point to an ant on the left.
- Point to an ant on the right.

Counting and Estimating

How well can your child count? Count to 10? Count to 20? Up to 100? Individual children will vary depending on home exposure. In school, your child will be expected to count. The Annie Ape ate ants picture plate presents many opportunities to ask questions about quantity. There are plenty of images to count in each of the picture plates.
- Count the apples.
- Count the ants.
- How many red apples are on the page? (5)
- How many yellow apples are on the page? (2)
- How many ants are in the **antwich**?
- How many apples have one bite taken out?
- How many apples are whole? How many apples have two bites taken out?
- How many apples have many bites taken out. How many apple cores are on the page?

- Show me an ant that is carrying an apple with two bites out of it.
- How many eyes does Annie have?
- How many eyes do the ants have?
- How many eyes can you see in the **antwich**?
- How many apples have only one leaf?
- How many apples have two leaves?
- How many apples are on the tree?
- How many apples are off the tree?
- How many ants are on the letter?
- How many ants are off the letter?
- How many leaves are on the tree?
- Show me a few ants.
- Show me many ants.

If your child has a good grasp of counting, the concept of estimating can be introduced. Estimating is a "ballpark" idea of about how many are on a page or in a letter or in a given area on a page. Estimating is always followed up with counting to see how close or how far from the actual number the estimate was.

- Show the page.
- After a few seconds take the page away.
- Ask your child, "About how many apples are on the tree?"

Make a mental note of the goodness of fit with the actual number.

If there are three (and there are), and your child says 4 or 5, that's reasonable.

If, on the other hand, your child says 50, you know that counting and quantity need more work. Also, you would hold off asking for estimates until a better grasp of numbers and quantity is established.

Memory and Phonemic Awareness

Each lesson has a memory training segment in three areas.

The visual area asks your child to look at the picture plate and recite the letter story. It then expects your child to be able to recite the letter story by looking at the letter card.

On the auditory level, your child recites the letter story by hearing the name of the letter. To develop phonological awareness, the child recites the letter story upon hearing the sound normally associated with the letter when we speak.

The final task is to recite all the letter stories up to and including the last one introduced.

For Annie Ape ate ants, you would show the picture plate and ask your child to recite the letter story.

Next, you would show the letter card **a**.

- What is the story? Next, say the name of the letter **a**. What is the story?
- Then, say the sound of the letter **a** as we hear it in the word hat.
- What is the letter story?

Finally, recite the stories in sequence.

Since this is the first letter, it is the only one that can be recited. Ultimately, all 26 letter stories will be recited, in sequence, without visual or auditory cues.

Note: Spend a few days working through each of the first few letter story plates. It will help you get comfortable with the depth and sequence of events. You probably won't get through every aspect of the lesson outline because your 20 to 30 minutes will fly by. Your child won't be able to concentrate beyond that time, either.

Benny Bear bakes buns

Drill Alphabet

Simply say, "Let's review the alphabet together." Present the letter cards and recite the name of each letter along with your child as each letter card is presented. If your child doesn't know the alphabet, repeat this exercise five times before moving on. If your child CAN recite the alphabet, do this once before going on to A-Z.

A-Z

Present the letter cards in order. Recite the names together as each card is presented. If your child is at the 95 percent accuracy level, conduct an individual checkout.

Z-A

If your child is at the 95 percent accuracy level A-Z, present the cards in reverse order (Z-A). Recite the names together as each card is presented. If this is a new exercise, you will want to conduct several repetitions.

Random Presentation for Developing Proficiency in Letter Name Recognition

If the level of accuracy Z-A is at the 95 percent level, take any source of print and have your child say the names of the letters as they appear in one or more sentences. Remember to provide closure for the exercise by reading the sentences.

Introduce Letter Story

- Introduce Benny Bear bakes buns.
- Drill to a level of functional recall.

Language Development and Visual Literacy

Present the picture plate for Benny Bear if not used when introducing the letter story.

Check out the meanings of the words used in the story and the vocabulary stimulated by the illustrations.
- What does bake mean?
- What is a bun?
- How is a bun different from a slice of bread? A loaf of bread?

Investigate your child's personal experience with bears, baking, and buns.
- Do you know another word for buns? (Rolls)
- Show me the burner.
- Show me the basket. What is in the basket? (bread, baguettes, bagels, croissants, buns)
- What is Benny wearing? (A bib. A chef's hat. Oven mitts.)
- Why is Benny wearing mitts?
- How do you know the buns are hot?
- What kind of a basket is holding the bread? (A reed basket. A bushel basket. A wicker basket.)
- Can bears really bake buns or bread?

Color

- What color is the letter **b**?
- Show me the pink oven mitts.
- What color is Benny's hat?
- Show me the bib. What color is it?
- What color is the basket?
- What color is the oven?

Comprehension

- What kind of animal is in the story?
- What is the bear's name?
- What does Benny do?
- What does Benny bake?
- Who bakes buns?
- What kind of buns does Benny bake? (Although the answer isn't contained in the story, it is a legitimate question that confirms understanding. So, the answer, it doesn't tell us, or it doesn't say, is appropriate.)

Word Boundaries and Word Identification

Review what we call the white spaces between words. (See explanation in the lesson for the letter a if needed.) The operative words in word identification are: Which word is…or show me…or point to.
- Which word is bear?
- Point to Benny.
- Show me the word bakes.
- Point to buns.

Spelling

- Spell bear. (b-e-a-r-)
- What word did you spell? (bear)
- Spell Benny.
- What word did you spell? (Benny)
- Spell bakes.
- What word did you spell? (bakes)
- Spell buns.
- What word did you spell? (buns)

Ordinals

Review the information on ordinals in the Introductory Notes to the Manual.

Maintain the following procedure until you sense your child is quite comfortable with the concept and the process used to drill it. Children thrive under predictable patterns of presentation, especially at ages 4 and 5.
- How many words are in the story? Count them.
- Benny is word number one.
- Bear is word number two.
- Bakes is word number three.
- Buns is word number four.
- Which is word number one? (Benny)
- Which is word number two? (Bear)
- Which is word number three? (bakes)
- Which is word number four? (buns).

How many words are in the story?
- Point to each word while saying one, two, three, and four.
- Do this several times.
- Verify understanding by asking which word is….one, two, three, four.
- Watch and listen again. One, two, three, four, while pointing to each word.
- After three or four repetitions, switch to first, second, third, fourth.
- Repeat several times.
- Say it with me.

Don't do "checkouts" until you are sure your child has a firm grasp of the concept. In my experience, I have found that it takes firm teaching between 10 to 15 letters before it becomes fully functional. Go slowly and carefully. Resist temptation to move too quickly.

Concepts

Paradigm concepts that can be considered for development in this picture plate include: half/whole; left/right; in/out; top/bottom; above/below; and small/large.
- Show me a whole loaf of bread.
- Show me half a loaf.
- Show me a whole bun.
- Show me a bun cut in half.
- Point to a pan of buns in the oven.
- Point to a pan of buns out of the oven.
- Show me a bread in the basket.
- Show me a bread out of the basket.
- Point to a bread above the **b**.
- Point to a bun below the **b**.
- Show me a bread at the top of the page.
- Show me one at the bottom of the page.
- Show me a large bun.
- Show me a small bun.

Counting and Estimating
- How many bagels are in the **b**?
- How many buns are in the **b**?
- How many loaves of bread are in the b? Out of the **b**?
- How many different breads/buns can you see in the basket?
- How many legs of the oven can you see?
- How many bagels are on the page?
- How many buns are on the page?
- How many loaves of bread are on the page?

Memory and Phonemic Awareness

Show the pictures **a** to **b**. Read letter stories.

Show cards **a** to **b**. Recite letter stories.
- Say letter names a.to b. Recite stories.
- Say letter sounds a to b. Recite stories.
- Let's recite the letter stories together from memory, **a** to **b**.
- Now you do it on your own.

Connie Cougar combs cubs

Drill Alphabet

Say to your child, "Let's review the alphabet." Present the letter cards saying the name as each is presented. If your child can't recite the alphabet, by rote, repeat this exercise five times. If your child can do it, move on to A-Z.

A-Z

Present the letter cards in order. Recite the names together as each card is presented. If your child is at the 95 percent accuracy level, conduct an individual checkout.

Z-A

If your child is at the 95 percent accuracy level A-Z, present the cards in reverse order (Z-A). Recite the names together as each card is presented. If this is a new exercise, conduct several repetitions.

Random Presentation for Developing Proficiency in Letter Name Recognition

When the level of accuracy Z-A is at the 95 percent level, take any source of print and have your child say the names of the letters as they appear in one or more sentences. Provide closure to the exercise by reading the sentences aloud.

Introduce Letter Story

- Introduce Connie Cougar combs cubs.
- Drill to a functional level of recall.

Language Development and Visual Literacy

Present the picture plate for Connie Cougar if not used when the letter story was introduced.

Check out the meanings of the words used in the story and the vocabulary stimulated by the illustrations.

- What is a cougar?
- Have you ever seen one? Where?
- What is a cub?
- How would a cougar really comb the cub's coat? Show me the picture.
- Where does a cougar live?
- What kind of tree is in the picture?
- Does a cougar eat cherries?
- Where could we find out what kind of food cougars eat?
- What kind of combs are in the picture?
- Show me a piece of chocolate cake.
- How do you know it is chocolate?
- Show me the cookies.
- What kind of decorations do they have?

Color

- Show me a green comb.
- Show me a blue tailcomb.
- Show me a yellow comb.
- Show me a red tailcomb.
- Show me a light grey animal.
- Show me a dark grey animal.
- Show me a yellow cookie.
- Show me an orange/brown cookie.
- Show me a pink tongue.
- What color is the letter **c**?
- What color is the cave?
- What color are the leaves on the tree?
- What is the color of the trunk?

Comprehension

- What does Connie do?
- Who combs cubs?
- What kind of animal is Connie?
- What does Connie comb?

Word Boundaries and Word Identification

Review word boundaries; what they are and what they do.

- How many words are in the story?
- How many word boundaries are in the story?
- Which word is combs?
- Point to Connie.
- Show me Cougar.
- Which word is cubs?

Spelling

- Spell combs
- What word did you spell?
- Spell Connie. What word did you spell?
- Spell Cougar. What word did you spell?
- Spell cubs. What word did you spell?

Ordinals

- Review the information on ordinals.
- Connie is word number one.
- Cougar is word number two.
- Combs is word number three.
- Cubs is word number four.

Point to each word while saying one, two, three, four.

- Do this a few times.
- Watch and listen.
- While pointing to each word, say, "One, two, three, four."
- Repeat this a few times and then switch to first, second, third, fourth.
- Repeat several times and then ask your child to say it with you.

Note: If you are sure that your child understands the concept of ordinals and has a reasonable chance of answering questions, successfully, conduct a checkout at this point. Otherwise, maintain the teaching of the concept up to the letter **g** before conducting a checkout. Because this is a cumulative process, it is counterproductive to forge ahead too quickly.

Concepts

Concepts that are opposites to consider in this plate include: above/below; in front of/in back of; single/pair; opened/closed; and light/dark.

- Show me the cougars that are above the **c**.
- Show me the combs that are below the **c**.
- Is the cave in front of the tree or in back of the tree?
- Show me a single cub.
- Show me a pair of cubs.
- Show me eyes that are opened.
- Show me eyes that are shut.
- Point to the piece of cake that is dark.
- Point to a piece of cake that is light.

Counting and Estimating

- How many cougars are on the page?
- How many cherries?
- How many of the cougars are cubs?
- How many combs are in the picture?
- Show the picture asking your child to look at it. Remove the picture from sight and ask, "About how many baked goods are in the **c**?"

Memory and Phonemic Awareness

- Show the picture plates from **a** to **c**. Ask your child to read the letter stories.
- Show the alphabet cards, **a** to **c**. Ask your child to recite the letter stories for each.
- Say the letter names, **a** to **c**. Ask your child to recite the letter stories.
- Say the sounds of the letters, **a** to **c**. Ask your child to recite the letter stories.
- Remove all cues. Recite the letter stories, in sequence, **a** to **c**.
- Have your child do it alone, with no cues.

Dewdney Dragon digs dungeons

Drill Alphabet

Simply say, "Let's review the alphabet together." Present the letter cards and recite the name of each letter along with your child as each letter card is presented. If your child doesn't know the alphabet, repeat this exercise five times before moving on in the lesson. If your child CAN recite the alphabet, do this once before going on to A-Z.

A-Z

Present the letter cards in order. Recite the names together as each card is presented. If your child is at the 95 percent accuracy level, conduct an individual checkout.

Z-A

If your child is at the 95 percent accuracy level A-Z, present the cards in reverse order (Z-A). Recite the names together as each card is presented. If this is a new exercise, you will want to conduct several repetitions. If your child is proficient, move on to random presentation.

Random Presentation for Developing Proficiency in Letter Name Recognition

If the level of accuracy Z-A is at the 95 percent level, take any source of print and have your child say the names of the letters as they appear in one or more sentences. Remember to provide closure for the exercise by reading the sentences aloud so that your child makes the connection between strings of letters and words and ideas.

Introduce Letter Story

- Introduce Dewdney Dragon digs dungeons.
- Drill to a level of functional recall.

Language Development and Visual Literacy

- Check out the meanings of the words used in the story.
- Check out the vocabulary concepts stimulated by the picture plate.
- What do we do with a shovel?
- Show me a dragon that is digging.
- Point to another one.
- What is a dungeon?
- Do dragons really exist? Are they alive?
- Where have you seen a dragon?
- Show me a door. Show me another one.
- What do the doors in this house look like?
- Are they shaped like these.
- Show me a window.
- What do the windows have on them?
- Why do we have stairs in our houses?
- Point to the pillar.
- Point to the ceiling.

Color

- What color is the dragon?
- What color is the door?
- What color is the shovel?
- What color is the **d**?
- What color are the stairs?
- Point to something yellow.
- Show me something black.
- Show me white.

Comprehension

- What does the dragon dig?
- What is the dragon's name?
- What is Dewdney?
- What does the dragon do?

Word Identification and Word Boundaries

Review word boundaries and the concept of word. Word boundaries define where a word begins and where a word ends. Show me... point to... and, which word is... are the operative words in word identification.

- Point to the word dungeon.
- Show me the word Dewdney.
- Which word is dragon?
- Show me the word digs.

Spelling

- Spell dungeon. What word did you spell?
- Spell Dewdney. What word did you spell?
- Spell dragon. What word did you spell?
- Spell digs. What word did you spell?

Ordinals

- How many words are in the story?
- Dewdney is word number one.
- Dragon is word number two.
- Digs is word number three.
- And, dungeons is word number four.
- Which is word number one? Point to it.
- Which is word number two? Point to it.
- Which is word number three? Point to it.
- Which is word number four? Point to it.
- Instead of saying word number one, I can say, "Which is the first word?"
- Instead of number two, I can say, second.
- Instead of word number three, I can say, third.
- And, instead of saying number four, I can say, fourth.
- Point to each word saying one, two, three, four.
- Repeat several times and switch to first, second, third, fourth.
- Say it with me.

Don't do checkouts until you are certain your child has a firm grasp of the concepts. Resist the temptation to move too quickly.

Concepts

The pairs of concepts embedded in the picture plate are: open/close; in/out; over/under; above/below; left/right,; and, top/bottom.

- Point to a door that is open.
- Point to a door that is closed.
- Which door is in the **d**?
- Which door is are out of the **d**?
- Show me a dragon that is over the **d**.
- Show me a door that is below the **d**.
- Point to the dragon on the left.
- Point to the dragon on the right.
- Show me a window on the left.
- Show me a window on the right.
- Point to a dragon at the top.
- Point to a dragon at the bottom.

Counting and Estimating

- How many dragons are having fun?
- How many doors are in the picture?
- How many windows?
- How many shovels are there?
- How many sets of stairs are there?
- Count the steps in the large set of stairs.
- Count the steps in the small set of stairs.
- How many **d**'s are in the picture?
- How many bars does each of the windows have?
- How many doors are closed?
- How many doors are open?
- How many pillars are there?

Memory and Phonemic Awareness

- Show the picture plates **a** to **d**. Ask your child to recite the stories.
- Show the alphabet cards **a** to **d**. Ask your child to recite the stories.
- Say the letter names **a** to **d**. Ask your child to recite the stories.
- Say the letter sounds **a** to **d**. Ask your child to recite the stories.
- Together, let's recite the letter stories **a** to **d**.
- Now you do it on your own.

Eadie Elk eats eggplants

Alphabet Drill

Let's review the alphabet together. Present the letter cards and recite the name of each letter along with your child as each letter card is presented. If your child doesn't know the alphabet, repeat this exercise five times before moving on in the lesson. If your child CAN recite the alphabet, go on to A-Z.

A-Z

Present the letter cards in order. Recite the names together as each card is presented. If your child is at the 95 percent level of accuracy, conduct an individual checkout.

Z-A

If your child is at the 95 percent accuracy level A-Z, present the cards in reverse order (Z-A). Recite the names together as each card is presented. If this is a new exercise, you will want to conduct several repetitions. Note the letters missed. If your child is proficient, do an individual checkout. If your child is at the 95 percent accuracy level, move on to random presentations.

Random Presentation for Developing Proficiency in Letter Name Recognition

If Z-A is at 95 percent or better, take any source of print and have your child say the names of the letters as they appear in one or more sentences, or a paragraph. Remember to provide closure to the exercise by reading the sentences aloud so that your child makes the connection between strings of letters and words and ideas.

Introduce Letter Story
- Introduce Eadie Elk eats eggplants.
- Drill to a level of functional recall.

Language Development and Visual Literacy

Check out the meanings of the words used in the story and enlarge your child's vocabulary through the illustration.
- What is eggplant?
- Have you ever tasted it?
- Does Mom cook it?
- How does it grow?
- What kind of egg is this? (Point to the fried egg.)
- And what kind is this one? (Point to a hard boiled egg cut in two.)
- And this one? (Point to the peeled, hard boiled egg.)
- Point to the painted eggs. What kind of eggs are these?
- Where do elk live?
- What happened to this egg? (Show the broken shell.)
- What did Eadie do to the fruit?
- Show me an eggplant that has fallen off the plant.
- Show me an envelope that has a stamp on it.
- What is on the easel? (The eye of Ra... from Egyptian mythology)
- What does the elk have on its head?
- What are they called?

Color
- What color is the fruit on the eggplant?
- What color is the plant, itself?
- Show me an egg with yellow on it.
- Point to a pink egg.
- Which eggs have stars on them?
- Show me an eggplant that has fallen off the plant.
- Can you show me another? Where?
- Is this one the same color as the other?
- Show me a green egg.
- Show me an egg that is white.
- What are the colors in the eye of Ra?
- What color is the stamp on the envelope?

Comprehension
- What does Eadie do?
- What does Eadie eat?
- What is the elk's name?
- What kind of an animal is Eadie?
- Who eats eggplant?

Word Identification and Word Boundaries
- Review word boundaries and their function.
- Point to eats.
- Which word is eggplants?
- Show me the word Eadie.
- Which word is Elk?

Spelling

- Spell eats.
  What word did you spell?
- Spell eggplants.
  What word did you spell?
- Spell Eadie.
  What word did you spell?
- Spell Elk.
  What word did you spell?

Ordinals

There are four words in the story. Eadie is word number one. Elk is word number two. Eats is word number three. And, eggplants is word number four.

- Point to word number one. What word is it?
- Point to word number two. What word is it?
- Point to word number three. What word is it?
- Point to word number four. What word is it?
- Point to each word saying, one, two, three, four.
- Repeat several times. Switch to first, second, third, fourth.
- After several repetitions, ask your child to say it along with you.

If your child is gaining proficiency and seems to have grasped the ordinal concept, hold off doing an individual checkout until the letter **g** is presented.

Concepts

- Show me an eggplant that is on the bush.
- Show me an eggplant that is off the bush.
- Show me the front of an envelope.
- Show me the back of an envelope.
- Show me an egg that is cut in half.
- Show me an egg that is whole.
- Show me an egg that is plain.
- Show me an egg that is decorated.
- Show me an eggplant that has a bite taken out of it.
- Show me an eggplant that is whole.

Counting and Estimating

- How many plants are in the picture?
- How many elk are there?
- How many decorated eggs are in the **e**?
- How many decorated eggs are out of the **e**?
- How many eggplants are on the bushes?
- How many eggplants are off the bushes?
- How many envelopes are in the **e**?
- How many fried eggs are in the **e**?
- How many hard boiled eggs are in the **e**?

Remove the picture from view before asking, "About how many objects are in the **e**?"

Memory and Phonemic Awareness

- Show the picture plates **a** to **e**. Ask your child to recite the letter stories.
- Show the alphabet cards **a** to **e**. Ask your child to recite the letter stories.
- Say the letter names **a** to **e**. Recite the letter stories.
- Say the letter sounds **a** to **e**. Recite the stories.
- Recite the letter stories from **a** to **e**, from memory. Say them together.
- Ask your child to recite the letter stories **a** to **e** alone, with no cues.

Freddy Fish follows flies

Alphabet Drill

If your child can recite the alphabet, by rote, go on to A-Z. If not, continue working toward rote recitation.

Present the letter cards and recite the name of each letter along with your child as each letter card is presented. If your child is still in the rote learning stage, repeat this exercise four or five times before moving on in the lesson.

A-Z

Present the letter cards in order. Recite the names together as each card is presented. If your child is at the 95 percent accuracy level, conduct an individual checkout by having your child say the names while you present the cards.

Z-A

If your child is at the 95 percent accuracy level A-Z, present the cards in reverse order (Z-A). Recite the names together as each card is presented. If this is a new exercise, you will want to conduct several repetitions. Note the letters misidentified. If your child is proficient, at the 95 percent accuracy level, do an individual checkout and move on to random presentations.

Random Presentation for Developing Proficiency in Letter Name Recognition

If the checkout for Z-A is at the 95 percent level, or better, take any source of print and have your child say the names of the letters as they appear in one or more sentences, or a paragraph. Provide closure to the exercise by reading the sentences, or the paragraph aloud. This will help your child make the connection between strings of letters, words, and ideas.

Introduce Letter Story

- Introduce Freddy Fish follows flies.
- Drill to a level of functional recall.

Language Development and Visual Literacy

Check out the meanings of the words used in the story and enlarge your child's vocabulary through the imagery in the illustration.

- Why is the fish following where the fly goes?
- What do frogs eat?
- What kind of a home is this fish living in? (fishbowl)
- Show me a flag with flies on it.
- Point to a flag with flowers.
- Which flag has a fish on it?
- What does the fourth flag have on it?
- How long is a frog's tongue?
- Point to the football. Ask what it is.
- What do you do with a football?
- How can you tell that the fish is happy that the fly is above the fishbowl?
- What is the frog with the short tongue doing?
- What do you do when you follow? What does it mean to follow?

Color

- What color is the football?
- What color is the water in the fishbowl?
- What color is the fish?
- What color is the frog?
- What color is the f?
- Point to the blue flag.
- Show me the red and green flag. What does it have on it?
- What color is the fly?
- What color is the frog's tongue?

Comprehension
- What kind of animal is in the story?
- What does the animal eat?
- What is the frog's name?
- What does the fish do?
- What does Freddy follow?

Word Identification and Word Boundaries
- Review word boundaries and their function.
- Point to fish.
- Point to flies.
- Which word is Freddy?
- Show me follows.
- How many word boundaries are in the story? (3)

Spelling
- Spell fish. What word did you spell?
- Spell flies. What word did you spell?
- Spell Freddy. What word did you spell?
- Spell follows. What word did you spell?

Ordinals
There are four words in the story. Freddy is word number one. Frog is word two. Follows is word three, and flies is word four.
- Point to each word saying one, two, three, four.
- Repeat this step several times and then switch to first, second, third, fourth.
- After several repetitions, ask your child to say it along with you.
- Even if your child seems proficient, wait till G for the checkout.

Counting and Estimating
Show the illustration. Withdraw the image and ask, "About how many flags are in the picture? Let's count them."

Show illustration again. Withdraw the image. About how many footballs are there on the page? Let's count them.
- How many fish are in the picture?
- Count the flies.
- How many frogs are there in the image?

Memory and Phonemic Awareness
- Show plates **a** to **f**. Ask your child to recite the stories.
- Show letter cards **a** to **f**. Ask your child to recite the stories.
- Say the letter names **a** to **f**. Ask your child to recite the stories.
- Say the letter sounds **a** to **f**. Ask your child to recite the stories.
- Recite the stories **a** to **f** together.
- Ask your child to recite the letter stories **a** to **f** without the use of visual or auditory cues.
- Prompt, where necessary.

Gertie Goose gathers gardenias

Drill Alphabet

If your child can recite the alphabet, by rote, go on to A-Z. If not, continue drilling for rote proficiency. Present the letter cards and recite the name of each letter along with your child as each letter card is presented. Repeat this exercise four or five times before moving on in the lesson.

A-Z

Present the letter cards in order. Recite the names together as each card is presented. When you sense your child is at the 95 percent proficiency level, conduct an individual checkout, where the child names each of the letters as they appear.

Z-A

If your child is at the 95 percent level in A-Z, present the cards in reverse order (Z-A). Recite the names together as each card is presented. If this is a relatively new exercise, several repetitions are in order. Note the letters misidentified. If your child is 95 percent proficient, conduct an individual checkout and move on to randomized letter presentations.

Random Presentation for Developing Proficiency in Letter Name Recognition

If Z-A is at 95 percent or better, take any source of print and have your child say the names of the letters as they appear in one or more sentences, or a paragraph. Read the sentences/paragraph aloud so your child can connect how letters form words, which combine to form sentences and paragraphs. Note speed of recognition. If it is slow, encourage faster recognition without inducing frustration. Increased speed of recognition should come along with increased familiarity with the letters.

Introduce Letter Story
- Introduce Gertie Goose gathers gardenias.
- Drill to a level of functional recall.

Language Development and Visual Literacy

Check out the meanings of the vocabulary of the story and the vocabulary stimulated by the imagery.
- What are gardenias?
- Have you ever seen a real one?
- Do they have a fragrant smell? Do they smell nice?
- What do you do when you gather things?
- Ask, "What do we call this?" while pointing to the garland.
- Do the same for trellis.
- Why do we have gates? Can you show me one?
- What do we call the fruit that is in the garland?
- What do we call these round things in the letter?
- What is it on top of the letter?
- What is Gertie going to do with the gardenias?
- What is Gertie wearing? (glasses, a hat)
- Does a real goose wear glasses? A hat?
- Does Gertie look happy or sad? How can you tell?
- Are grapes good to eat?
- What do we make with grapes?

Color
- What color is the letter?
- What color is Gertie?
- Point to the gate. What color is it?
- What color are the ribbons on the garland?
- Name the colors of the gumballs, starting here.
- What color are Gertie's feet and beak?
- What color is her hat?
- What color are the grapes?
- What color are gardenias?
- What color is the trellis? Do you remember what a trellis is?

Comprehension
- What is the story? Gertie Goose gathers gardenias.
- What is the goose's name?
- What does Gertie do?
- What kind of animal is Gertie?
- What does Gertie gather?
- Who gathers gardenias?
- Why does she gather gardenias? (That is information not contained in the story. Conveys comprehension.)

Word Identification, Word Boundaries, Spelling.

Word boundaries define where a word begins and ends. Show me... point to... and, which word is... are the operative words in word identification. How many word boundaries are in the story?

- Point to the word, Gertie. Spell it. What word did you spell?
- Which word is gathers? Spell gathers. What word did you spell?
- Show me the word goose. Spell it. What word did you spell?
- Which word is gardenias? Spell gardenias. What word did you spell?

Ordinals

- How many words are in the story?
- Gertie is word one.
- Goose is word two.
- Gathers is word three.
- Gardenias is word four.
- One, two, three, four. Point to the words while saying one, two, three, four.
- Instead of saying word number one, I can say first.
- Instead of saying word number two, I can say second.
- Instead of saying word number three, I can say third.
- Instead of saying word number four, I can say fourth.
- Point to the words while saying, first, second, third, fourth.
- Do this several times.
- Now ask, "Show me the first word." What word is it?
- Show me the second word.
- Show me the third word.
- Show me the fourth word.
- What word is the third word? Gathers.
- What word is the first word? Gertie
- What word is the fourth word? Gardenias
- What word is the second word? Goose.

Concepts

- Are the bows at the top of the page or the bottom of the page?
- Point to a large gumball.
- Point to a small gumball.

- Where is the gumball machine? On the letter or off the letter?
- Where is Gertie putting the gardenias? (in the bowl)
- Run your finger along the gumballs to show me they are getting larger.
- Show me how they are getting smaller?
- Show me the gardenias that are on the bush.
- Show me the gardenias that are off the bush.

Counting and Estimating

- How many gardenias are on the bush?
- How many gates are there?
- How many gumballs are in the **g**? Count them.
- How many feet does Gertie have?
- How many bows?
- How many clusters of grapes? Count them.
- How many bows are on the garland?

Memory and Phonemic Awareness

- Show the plates **a** to **g**. Recite the stories.
- Show cards **a** to **g**. Recite the stories.
- Say letter names **a** to **g**. Recite the stories.
- Say the letter sounds **a** to **g**. Recite the stories.
- Recite the stories **a** to **g**, together, without cues.
- Ask the child to recite the stories **a** to **g**, alone, without cues.
- Prompt, where necessary.

Harley Hamster hates hawks

Drill Alphabet

If your child can recite the alphabet, by rote, go on to A-Z. If not, continue drilling for rote proficiency. Present the letter cards and recite the name of each letter along with your child as each letter is presented. Repeat this exercise four or five times before moving on in the lesson.

A-Z

Present the letter cards in order. Recite the names together as each card is presented. When you sense your child is at the 95 percent proficiency level, conduct an individual checkout, where the child names each of the letters as they appear.

Z-A

If your child is at the 95 percent level in A-Z, present the cards in reverse order (Z-A). Recite the names together as each card is presented. If this is a relatively new exercise, several repetitions are in order. Note the letters misidentified. If your child is 95 percent proficient, conduct an individual checkout and move on to randomized letter presentations.

Random Presentation for Developing Proficiency in Letter Name Recognition

If Z-A is at the 95 percent level or better, take any source of print and have your child say the names of the letters as they appear in one or more sentences, or a paragraph. Read the sentences/paragraph aloud so your child can connect how letters form words, which combine to form sentences and paragraphs. Note speed of recognition. If it is slow, encourage faster recognition without inducing frustration. Increased speed of recognition should follow increased familiarity with the letters.

Introduce Letter Story

- Introduce Harley Hamster hates hawks.
- Drill to a level of functional recall.

Language Development and Visual Literacy

Check out the vocabulary of the story along with the vocabulary suggested in the illustration.
- What is a hamster? Show me the hamster on the page.
- Show me the hawk.
- Why does Harley hate the hawk?
- Choose a hat. Point to it. Who would wear that kind of hat?
- Point to the helmets. What do we call these kinds of hats?
- What do helmets do?
- Select the visor helmet. Who would wear this kind of helmet?
- What about this one? Point out the gladiator helmet.
- Do the same for the football helmet.
- Show me the motorcycle.
- Why is Harley mad?
- What is that coming from the chimney of the house?
- What is the hawk standing on?
- What is the wheel doing up in the tree?
- Does it belong on the motorcycle? Why not?

Color

- What color is the hawk?
- What color is the motorcycle?
- Point to the pink helmet.
- Point to the yellow helmet.
- Show me a blue hat.
- Show me a green hat.
- Show me a black tophat.
- Show me a blue football helmet.
- Show me a green gladiator helmet.
- What color is the house?

Comprehension

- What does the hamster do? (hates)
- What does he hate?
- What kind of animal is Harley?
- What is the hamster's name?

Word Identification, Word Boundaries, Spelling

Review word boundaries and their function to identify where a word begins and ends.
- Point to hates. Spell hates.
  What word did you spell?
- Point to hawks. Spell hawks.
  What word did you spell?
- Which word is hamster?
  Spell hamster. What word did you spell?
- Which word is Harley?
  Spell Harley. What word did you spell?

Ordinals

- How many word boundaries are there in the story?
- How many words are in the story?
- Harley is word one.
- Hamster is word two.
- Hates is word three.
- Hawks is word four.
- Point to the words while saying one, two, three, four.
- Repeat that several times and then switch to first, second, third, fourth.
- What is the first word? (Harley)
- What is the second word?
- What is the third word?
- What is the fourth word?
- Show me the third word.
- How do you spell the second word?
- Which word tells me the name of the hamster, the first, second, third, or fourth word? (first)

Provide this kind of variation only if the proficiency level is good and you know that the child will be able to figure it out.

Concepts

- Show me the hat over the **h**.
- Show me the hat under the **h**.
- Which animal has an open mouth?
- Which animal has a closed mouth?
- Which animal is looking up?
- Which animal is looking down?

- Which animal is standing?
- Which animal is sitting?

Counting and Estimating

- How many hats are on the page?
- How many animals are on the page?
- How many buildings are in the picture?
- How many helmets are in the **h**?
- How many football helmets are there?
- How many cowboy hats are in the illustration?
- How many of the hats are gladiator hats?
- How many are motorcycle helmets?
- How many leaves are on the branch?

Memory and Phonemic Awareness

- Show the picture plates, **a** to **h**. Recite the stories.
- Show the letter cards, **a** to **h**. Recite the stories.
- Say the letter names, **a** to **h**. Recite the stories.
- Say the letter sounds, **a** to **h**. Recite the stories.
- Together, recite the letter stories, **a** to **h**, from memory.
- Child recites the stories, **a** to **h**, from memory.

Iris Iguana ignores insects

Alphabet Drill

If your child can recite the alphabet, by rote, go on to A-Z. If not, continue drilling for rote proficiency. Present the letter cards and recite the name of each letter along with your child as each letter card is presented. Repeat this exercise four or five times before moving on in the lesson.

A-Z

Present the letter cards in order. Recite the names together as each card is presented. When you sense your child is at the 95 percent proficiency level, conduct an individual checkout, where the child names each of the letters as they appear.

Z-A

If your child is at the 95 percent level in A-Z, present the cards in reverse order (Z-A). Recite the names together as each card is presented. If this is a relatively new exercise, several repetitions are in order. Note the letters misidentified. If your child is 95 percent proficient, conduct an individual checkout and move on to randomized letter presentations.

Random Presentation for Developing Proficiency in Letter Name Recognition

If Z-A is at 95 percent or better, take any source of print and have your child say the names of the letters as they appear in one or more sentences, or a paragraph. Read the sentences/paragraph aloud so your child can connect how letters for words, which combine to form sentences and paragraphs. Note speed of recognition. If it is slow, encourage faster recognition without inducing frustration. Increased speed of recognition should come along with increased familiarity with the letters.

Introduce Letter Story

- Introduce Iris Iguana ignores insects.
- Drill to a functional level of recall.

Language Development and Visual Literacy

Check out the meanings of the vocabulary of the story and that stimulated by the illustration. Note that Iguanas eat fruit, flowers and leaves. Most other lizards eat insects. The green iguanas are in danger of extinction because the young are collected and sold as pets. This storyline is based in reality.

- What does ignore mean? What do you do when you ignore someone or something?
- What are insects? What is another word we use to describe them?
- Why does Iris Iguana ignore the insects?
- Do you know someone who has a pet Iguana?

Color

- What is the color of the letter **i**?
- Show me a green and yellow ice cream cone.
- Show me a black ant.
- Show me a red ant.
- Show me a white and yellow ice cream cone.
- Show me the iguana with the red mouth.
- Show me something that is purple. What is it?
- Show me a red and yellow cone.
- Show me the insect that is purple and yellow. What is it?
- What color are the iguana's ears?
- What color is the iguana?
- What color are cherries?

Comprehension

- Tell me the story for **i**.
- What kind of animal is in the story?
- What is the animal's name?
- What does Iris do?
- What does Iris ignore?

Word Identification, Word Boundaries, Spelling

Word boundaries define where a word begins and ends. Show me...point to...which word is...are the operative words in word identification. How many word boundaries are in the story?

- Which word is iguana. Spell it. What word did you spell?
- Show me Iris. Spell it. What word did you spell?
- Point to ignores. Spell it. What word did you spell?
- Point to insects. Spell it. What word did you spell?

Ordinals

- How many words are in the story?
- Iris is word one.
- Iguana is word two.
- Ignores is word three.
- Insects is word four.
- Point to the words while saying one, two, three, four.
- Repeat a few times.
- Instead of saying word number one, what can I say?
- And for word number two, what could I say?
- And for word number three?
- And number four?
- Point to the words while saying, first, second, third, fourth.
- Repeat several times.
- Say, "Show me the first word." What word is it?
- Do the same for second through fourth.
- What word is the third word?
- What word is the fourth word?
- What word is the second word?
- What word is the first word?

Concepts

- Point to the iguana with an open mouth.
- Show me the iguana with a closed mouth.
- Point to the iguana in the tree.
- Show me the iguana out of the tree.
- Show me the iguana on the rock.
- Point to the iguana on the branch.
- Where is the butterfly? (on the iguana)
- Look at the top of the page, then look at the bottom of the page.
- Which iguana is asleep?
- Which iguana is awake?
- Show me the insect that is above the iguana.
- Show me the insect that is below the rock.
- Tell me the names of the fruit on the tree.
- Show me the insect that is above the iguana on the rock.
- Show me the insect that is crawling on the rock.
- Show me the insect that is flying below the iguana in the tree.

Counting and Estimating

- How many ice cream cones are in the **i**?
- How many ants are on the page?
- How many are black ants?
- How many butterflies are on the page?
- How many iguanas are there?
- Is there one fly, or more than one fly?
- Are there more iguanas or more ice cream cones?
- Are there more grapes or more cherries?
- Are there fewer apples or fewer grapes?
- Look at the page. Remove from sight.
- About how many cones are in the **i**?

Memory and Phonemic Awareness

- Show illustrations **a** to **i**. Recite the stories.
- Show cards **a** to **i**. Recite the stories.
- Say letter names **a** to **i**. Recite the stories.
- Say the letter sounds **a** to **i**. Recite the stories.
- Recite the stories **a** to **i**, together, without cues.
- Ask the child to recite the letter stories **a** to **i**, alone, without cues.
- Prompt, where necessary.

Jimmy Jackal juggles jellybeans

Alphabet Drill

If your child can recite the alphabet, by rote, go on to A-Z. If not, continue drilling for rote proficiency. Present the letter cards and recite the name of each letter along with your child as each letter is presented. Repeat this exercise four or five times before moving on in the lesson.

A-Z

Present the letter cards in order. Recite the names together as each card is presented. When you sense your child is at the 95 percent proficiency level, conduct an individual checkout, where the child names each of the letters as they appear.

Z-A

If your child is at the 95 percent level in A-Z, present the cards in reverse order (Z-A). Recite the names together as each card is presented. If this is a relatively new exercise, several repetitions are in order. Make a note of the letters misidentified. If your child is 95 percent proficient, conduct an individual checkout and move on to randomized letter presentations.

Random Presentation for Developing Proficiency in Letter Name Recognition

If Z-A is at 95 percent or better, take any source of print and have your child say the names of the letters as they appear in one or more sentences, or a paragraph. Read the sentences/paragraph aloud so your child can connect how letters form words, which combine to form sentences and paragraphs. Note the speed of recognition. If it is slow, encourage faster recognition without inducing frustration. Increased speed of recognition should come along with increased familiarity with the letters.

Introduce Letter Story

- Introduce Jim Jackal juggles jellybeans.
- Drill to a functional level of recall.

Language Development and Visual Literacy

Check out the meanings of the vocabulary of the story and that stimulated by the illustration.
- What do you do when you juggle?
- What is a jackal?
- Show me a jack-o-lantern.
- What is a jack-o-lantern made from?
- While pointing at the jack-in-the-box, ask what it is.
- How does a jack-in-the-box work?
- Point to the jigsaw puzzle pieces. Ask, "What are these?"
- Where are the jellybeans? (On the floor, on the table, in the jar, and in the air.)

Color

- What color is Jimmy?
- What color is the **j**?
- What color is the jack-o-lantern?
- What color is Jack?
- What color is the jar?
- Point to a green jellybean.
- Show me a red one.
- Show me a yellow one.
- Show me blue jar.
- Show me something purple.

Comprehension

- Tell me the story for **j**.
- What is the jackal's name?
- What does the jackal juggle?
- What does the jackal do?
- What kind of animal is Jimmy?
- What does Jimmy Jackal do?
- Who juggles jellybeans?

Word Identification, Word Boundaries, and Spelling

Word boundaries define where a word begins and ends. Show me...point to...which word is...are the operative words in word identification. How many words are in the story? How many word boundaries are in the story?
- Which word is Jimmy? Spell it. What word did you spell?

- Which word is jellybeans? Spell it. What word did you spell?
- Which word is juggles? Spell it. What word did you spell?
- Which word is Jackal? Spell it. What word did you spell?

Ordinals
- How many words are in the story?
- Jimmy is the first word.
- Jackal is the second word.
- Juggles is the third word.
- Jellybeans is the fourth word.
- Point to the words saying one, two, three, four.
- Repeat a few times.
- What word could I use instead of saying word number one?
- What word could I say instead of word number two?
- And for word number three?
- And number four?
- Point to the words saying first, second, third, and fourth.
- Repeat several times.
- Say, "Show me the first word." What word is it?
- Do the same for second through fourth.
- Repeat using random order.

Concepts
- Show me jellybeans in the jar.
- Show me jellybeans out of the jar.
- Show me jellybeans on the table.
- Show me jellybeans on the floor.
- Show me jellybeans in the air.
- Show me jigsaw puzzle pieces in the **j**.
- Show me jigsaw puzzle pieces in the dot of the **j**.
- Show me the jack on the box.
- Show me the jack in the air.
- Show me a jack-o-lantern on the left.
- Show me one on the right.
- Show me a jellybean to the left of the jar.
- Show me a jellybean to the right of the jar.

Counting and Estimating
- How many jellybeans are in the air?
- How many are on the floor?
- How many jellybeans are on the table?
- How many can you see in the jar?
- How many jellybeans are on the page? Count them.
- How many jack-o-lanterns are on the page?
- About how many jigsaw pieces are in the **j**?
- How many spots are on the jackal's nose?
- How many spots are on the jackal's back?
- How many figures are smiling?

Memory and Phonemic Awareness
- Show the illustrations **a** to **j**. Recite the stories.
- Show cards **a** to **j**. Recite the stories.
- Say letter names **a** to **j**. Recite the stories.
- Say the letter sounds **a** to **j**. Recite the stories.
- Recite the stories **a** to **j**, together, without cues.
- Ask the child to recite the letter stories **a** to **j**, alone, without cues.
- Prompt, where necessary.

Kelly Koala kicks kiwis

Alphabet Drill

If your child can recite the alphabet, by rote, go on to A–Z. If not, continue drilling for rote proficiency. Present letter cards and recite the name of each letter along with your child as each letter card is presented. Repeat this exercise four or five times before moving on in the lesson.

A-Z

Present the letter cards in order. Recite the names together as each card is presented. When you sense your child is at the 95 percent proficiency level, conduct an individual checkout, where the child names each of the letters as they appear.

Z-A

If your child is at the 95 percent level in A–Z, present the cards in reverse order Z–A. Recite the names together as each card is presented. If this is a relatively new exercise, several repetitions are in order. Make a note of the letters misidentified. If your child is 95 percent proficient, conduct an individual checkout and move on to random letter presentation.

Random Presentation for Developing Proficiency in Letter Name Recognition

If Z–A is at 95 percent or better, take any source of print and have your child say the names of the letters as they appear in one or more sentences, or a paragraph. Read the sentences/paragraph aloud so your child can connect how letters form words, which combine to form sentences and paragraphs. Note the speed of recognition. If it is slow, encourage faster recognition without inducing frustration. Increased speed of recognition should come along with increase familiarity with the letters.

Introduce Letter Story
- Introduce Kelly Koala kicks kiwis.
- Drill to a functional level of recall.

Language Development and Visual Literacy

Check out the meanings of the words in the story and the vocabulary stimulated by the illustration. Discuss your child's experiences with kiwis, koala bears, kangaroos, kites, and keys.
- To whom is Kelly kicking the kiwi?
- What do we call a baby kangaroo?
- Where does the joey live?
- What does a koala eat?
- What does a kiwi fruit look like on the outside?
- What does it look like on the inside?
- Who is going to catch the kiwi?
- What does the joey have on his hand?
- What are the differences between a skeleton key and a conventional key?
- Is a Koala bear a real bear?

Color
- Show me a red and yellow kite.
- Show me a yellow key.
- Show me an orange key.
- Show me a red kite.
- Show me a blue key.
- Show me a brown kiwi.
- Show me a green kiwi.
- Show me something that is grey and white. What is it?
- What color are the ears of the animals in the story?

Comprehension
- Tell me the story for **k**.
- What does Kelly kick?
- What does Kelly do?
- What is the Koala's name?
- What kind of animal is Kelly?
- What does Kelly Koala do?
- Who kicks kiwis?

Word Identification, Word Boundaries, Spelling

Word boundaries define where a word begins and ends. Show me…point to…which word is…are the operative words in word identification. How many words are in the story? How many word boundaries are in the story?

- Which word is kiwis. Spell it. What word did you spell?
- Which word is kicks? Spell it. What word did you spell?
- Which word is Kelly? Spell it. What word did you spell?
- Which word is Koala? Spell it. What word did you spell?

Ordinals

- Kelly is the first word. What is the first word?
- Koala is the second word. What is the second word?
- Kicks is the third word. What is the third word?
- Kiwis is the fourth word. What is the fourth word?
- Point while saying, first, second, third, fourth.
- Repeat a few times.
- Now you do it. (First, second, third, fourth)
- What word is kiwis?
- What word is kicks?
- What word is Kelly?
- What word is Koala?

Remember to reteach the concept of ordinals if a long interval of time has lapsed between drills. If you are just now introducing the concept of ordinals, be sure to study this sub-section in previous lessons.

Concepts

- Point to the key above the red and black key.
- Point to the key below the red and black key.
- Point to the key below the red and yellow kite.
- Point to the key above the red kite.
- Point to the animal on the left.
- Point to the animal on the right.
- Point to the kite in the tree.
- Point to a kite out of the tree.
- Point to a kiwi on Kelly's foot.
- Point to a kiwi off Kelly's foot.

Counting and Estimating

- How many kites are there?
- How many kiwis are on the page?
- How many animals are on the page?
- How many keys are in the **k**?
- About how many objects are in the **k**?

Memory and Phonemic Awareness

- Show illustrations **a** to **k**. Recite stories.
- Show cards **a** to **k**. Recite stories.
- Say letter names, **a** to **k**. Recite stories.
- Say letter sounds, **a** to **k**. Recite stories.
- Recite stories, **a** to **k**, together, without cues.
- Ask the child to recite the stories **a** to **k**, without cues, prompting, if necessary.

Leo Lion Licks Lollipops

Alphabet Drill

If your child can recite the alphabet, by rote, go on to A–Z. If not, continue drilling for rote proficiency. (Many children are proficient by this point.)

Present the letter cards and recite the name of each letter along with your child as each letter card is presented. Repeat this exercise four or five times before moving on to the next segment in the lesson.

A–Z

Present the letter cards in order. Recite the names together as each card is presented. When you sense that your child is at the 95 percent proficiency level, conduct an individual checkout where the child names each of the letters as they appear. (The children who can recite the alphabet, by rote, usually carry the rote forward into this exercise. That is why the reverse order checkout is significant.)

Z–A

If your child is at the 95 percent level in A-Z, present the cards in reverse order Z-A. Recite the names together as each card is presented. If this is a new exercise, several repetitions are in order. If this is a relatively easy exercise for your child, do it once together before the individual checkout, and then move on to the next segment.

Random Presentation for Developing Proficiency in Letter Name Recognition

If Z–A is proficient (95 percent or better), take any source of print and have your child say the names of the letters as they appear in one or more sentences, or a paragraph. Read the sentences/paragraph aloud so your child can connect how letters form words, which combine to form sentences and paragraphs. Make a note of the speed of recognition. If it is slow, encourage faster recognition without inducing frustration. Increased speed of recognition should follow naturally with increased familiarity.

Introduce Letter Story

- Introduce Leo Lion licks lollipops.
- Drill to a functional level of recall.

Language Development and Visual Literacy.

Check out the meanings of the words in the story and the vocabulary stimulated by the illustrations. Discuss your child's experiences with the animals and other aspects of the story and illustration.

- What is another word for lollipop?
- Show me a lion.
- Show me a lemon.
- Show me a lime.
- What do we call the category of fruit for lemons, limes, and grapefruits?
- What is another fruit that belongs in the category?
- How is an orange different from a lemon?
- Which fruit is sweet? An orange or a lime?
- Do lollipops grow on trees?
- Would a lion lick a lollipop?

Color

- Show me a lemon. What color is it?
- Show me a lime. What color is it?
- Show me a yellow and red lollipop.
- Show me a blue lollipop.
- What color is the lollipop that the lion is licking?

Comprehension

- What is the story for l?
- What does the lion do?
- What kind of animal is in the story?
- What is the lion's name?
- What does Leo lick?
- Who licks lollipops?
- What does Leo Lion lick?

Word Identification, Word Boundaries, Spelling

Word boundaries define where a word begins and ends. Show me…point to…which word is…are the operative words in word identification. How many words are in the story? How many word boundaries are in the story?

- Show me licks. Spell it. What word did you spell?
- Show me Lion. Spell it. What word did you spell?
- Show me Leo. Spell it. What word did you spell?
- Show me lollipops. Spell it. What word did you spell?

Ordinals
- First, second, third, fourth.
- Leo is the first word.
- Lion is the second word.
- Licks is the third word.
- Lollipops is the fourth word.

First, second, third, fourth. Point to each word as you say, first, second, third, fourth.

If this is a relatively familiar exercise, the amount of time spent in review of the concept can be shortened.

If this is a new exercise for your child, review the procedure established in the first few lessons using the current letter story to work the concept of ordinals.
- What is the third word?
- What is the first word?
- What is the fourth word?
- What is the second word?

At this point, you might want to introduce "last" as the equivalent for fourth.

Concepts
- Show me a lollipop in the tree.
- Show me a lollipop in the lion's paw.
- Show me a lion on a log.
- Show me a lion off the log.
- Show me a lion sitting.
- Show me a lion standing.
- Show me a whole lime.
- Show me a whole lemon.
- Show me a part of a lime.
- Show me a part of a lemon.
- Show me half a lemon.
- Show me half a lime.
- Show me a paw that is up.
- Show me a paw that is down.
- Show me a lollipop that is striped.
- Show me a lollipop that is solid.

Counting and Estimating
- How many lemons are on the page?
- How many lions are on the page?
- How many limes are on the page?
- How many lollipops are on the page?
- How many different greens are on the page?
- How many different browns are on the page?
- How many l's are on the page?
- About how many objects are in the l? (Show the page. Remove the page. Ask the question.)

Memory and Phonemic Awareness
- Show illustrations **a** to **l**. Recite the stories.
- Show cards **a** to **l**. Recite the stories.
- Say letter names **a** to **l**. Recite the stories.
- Say the letter sounds **a** to **l**. Recite the stories.
- Recite the stories **a** to **l**, together, without cues.
- Ask the child to recite the letter stories **a** to **l**, without cues, prompting where necessary.

Molly Moose makes music

Alphabet Drill

If your child can recite the alphabet, by rote, go on to A-Z. If not, continue drilling for rote proficiency. (Many children are proficient by this point.)

Present the letter cards and recite the name of each letter along with your child as each letter card is presented. Repeat this exercise four or five times before moving on to the next segment in the lesson.

A-Z

Present the letter cards in order. Recite the names together as each card is presented. When you sense that your child is at the 95 percent proficiency level, conduct an individual checkout. The child names each of the letters as they appear. (Children who can recite the alphabet, by rote, usually carry the rote forward into this exercise.) If your child is proficient, do it once together before the individual checkout.

Z-A

If your child is proficient in A-Z, present the cards in reverse order Z-A. Recite the names together as each card is presented. If this is a new exercise, several repetitions are in order. If this is a relatively easy exercise for your child, do it once together before the individual checkout. Then move on to the next segment in the lesson.

Random Presentation for Developing Proficiency in Letter Name Recognition

If Z-A is proficient at the 95 percent level or better, take any source of print and have your child say the names of the letters as they appear in one or more sentences, or a paragraph. Read the sentences/paragraph aloud so your child can connect how letters form words, which combine to form sentences and paragraphs. Make a note of the speed of recognition. If it is slow, encourage faster recognition without inducing frustration. Increased speed of recognition follows naturally with increased familiarity.

Introduce Letter Story

- Introduce Molly Moose makes music.
- Drill to a functional level of recall.

Language Development and Visual Literacy

Check out the meanings of the words in the story and the vocabulary stimulated by the illustrations. Discuss your child's experiences with the animals and other aspects of the illustration.

Molly is holding a baton in her hand. That means that she is the conductor of the orchestra. What is a conductor?
- What kind of tie is Molly wearing?
- Who is sitting on the mushroom?
- What instrument is the penguin playing?
- What instrument is the rat playing?
- What is Leo playing?
- Who is the soloist? (Yonita Yak)
- What is the yak singing into?
- What is on the music stand?
- What is Molly holding in her hand?
- Show me the staff.
- Show me a staff with musical notes.
- Who plays a musical instrument in your family?

Color

- What color is Molly?
- What color is her jacket?
- What color is her tie?
- What color is her shirt?
- What color is the mushroom the penguin is sitting on?
- What color is the yak?
- What color is the **m**?
- What color is the rat?
- What color is the piano?
- What color is the trumpet?
- What color is the microphone?
- What color is the drum?

Comprehension

- What is the story for **m**?
- What kind of animal is in the story?
- What is the animal's name?
- What does Molly make?
- What does Molly do?
- Who makes music?

- What does Molly Moose make?

Word Identification, Word Boundaries, Spelling

Word boundaries define where a word begins and ends. How many words are in the story? How many word boundaries are in the story?
- Which word is Moose?
  Spell it.
  What word did you spell?
- Which word is Molly?
  Spell it.
  What word did you spell?
- Which word is music?
  Spell it.
  What word did you spell?
- Which word is makes?
  Spell it.
  What word did you spell?

Ordinals

If this is a new exercise for your child, review the procedure established in the first few lessons. Use the current story to work the concept.

If your child is relatively familiar with ordinals, the amount of time spent in review of the concept can be shortened.

If your child is quite proficient, and you feel inclined to do so, ordinals can be incorporated into the previous segment. (e.g. What is the second word? Moose. Spell it. What word did you spell? Or Show me the second word. What word is it? Spell it. What word did you spell?)
- What is the third word?
- What is the first word?
- What is the second word?
- What is the fourth word?
- What is the last word?

Concepts
- Show me an animal sitting on the **m**.
- Show me an animal under the **m**.
- Show me some notes on the staff.
- Show me some notes off the staff.
- Show me some notes in the **m**.
- Show me some notes out of the **m**.
- Where is the lion?
- Where is the penguin sitting?
- Point to an animal at the bottom of the page.
- Point to an animal at the top of the page.
- Point to an animal at the left of the page.
- Show me an animal on the right.

Counting and Estimating
- How many animals are on the page?
- How many instruments are on the page?
- How many legs are on the music stand?
- How many musical notes are in the **m**?
- How many musical notes are out of the **m**?
- How many trumpets are there?
- How many pianos?
- How many drums?
- How many singers?

Memory and Phonemic Awareness
- Show illustrations **a** to **m**. Recite stories.
- Show cards **a** to **m**. Recite Stories
- Say letter names, **a** to **m**. Recite stories.
- Say letter sounds, **a** to **m**. Recite stories.
- Recite the stories **a** to **m**, together, without cues.
- Ask the child to recite the letter stories **a** to **m**, without cues. Prompt, if necessary.

Nellie Nag needs noodles

Alphabet Drill

If your child can recite the alphabet, by rote, go on to A-Z. If not, continue drilling for rote proficiency. (Many children are proficient at rote recitation by this point.)

Present the letter cards and recite the name of each letter along with your child as each letter card is presented. Repeat this exercise four or five times before moving on to the next segment in the lesson.

A-Z

Present the letter cards in order. Recite the names together as each card is presented. When you sense that your child is at the 95 percent proficiency level, conduct an individual checkout. The child names each of the letters as they appear. (The children who can recite the alphabet, by rote, usually carry the rote forward into this exercise.) If your child is proficient, do it once together before the individual checkout.

Z-A

If your child is proficient in A-Z, present the cards in reverse order Z-A. Recite the names together as each card is presented. If this is a new exercise, several repetitions are in order. If this is a relatively easy task for your child, do it once together before the individual checkout. Then move on to the next segment in the lesson.

Random Presentation for Developing Proficiency in Letter Name Recognition

If Z-A is proficient at the 95 percent level or better, take any source of print and have your child say the names of the letters as they appear in one or more sentences, or a paragraph. Read the sentences/paragraph aloud so your child can connect how letters form words, which combine to form sentences and paragraphs. Make a note of the speed of recognition. If it is labored, encourage faster recognition without inducing frustration. Increased speed of recognition follows naturally with increased familiarity with the alphabet.

Introduce Letter Story
- Introduce Nellie Nag needs noodles.
- Drill to a functional level of recall.

Language Development and Visual Literacy

Check out the meanings of the words in the story. Check out the vocabulary stimulated by the illustration. Discuss your child's experiences with the animals and other aspects of the illustration.
- What is a nag?
- Why do we call it a nag?
- Would a horse eat noodles?
- How do you make noodles?
- Point to the neckties and ask, "What are these?"
- Who wears them?
- How can you tell that Nellie Nag likes noodles?
- What are polka dots? Why are they called polka dots?
- What is written in the notebook?
- Who sews buttons on your clothes when they fall off?
- Show me a polka dotted necktie.
- Show me a striped necktie.
- Show me a plain necktie.
- Show me one with a patch on it.

Colors
- What color is Nellie?
- What color is the **n**?
- Name the colors in the ties.
- What color is the table.
- Name the colors of the bowls.

Comprehension
- What is the story for **n**?
- What is the horse's name?
- What does the horse need?
- What kind of animal is Nellie?
- What does Nellie do?

Word Identification, Word Boundaries, Spelling

Word boundaries define where a word begins and ends. How many words are in the story? How many word boundaries are in the story? What is a word boundary?

- Which word is Nellie? Spell it. What word did you spell?
- Which word is noodles? Spell it. What word did you spell?
- Which word is Nag? Spell it. What word did you spell?
- Which word is needs? Spell it. What word did you spell?

Ordinals

If this is a new exercise for your child, review the procedure established in the first few lessons. Use the current letter story to work the concept.

If your child is familiar with ordinals, the amount of time spent in review of the concept can be shortened.

If your child is quite proficient, and you feel inclined to do so, ordinals can be incorporated into the previous segment. (e.g., What is the first word? Spell it. What word did you spell?)

- What is the first word?
- What is the fourth word?
- What is the second word?
- What is the third word?

Concepts

- Point to the bowl of noodles on the table.
- Show me the bowl on the **n**.
- Show me a bowl in the **n**.
- What is the horse wearing around her neck?
- What is the horse leaning against?
- What numbers are on the left page of the notebook?
- What numbers are on the right page of the notebook?
- What numbers are in the top right?
- What numbers are in the top left?
- What numbers are in the bottom right?
- What numbers are in the bottom left?

Counting and Estimating

- How many ties are in the picture?
- How many bowls of noodles are in the picture?
- How many bowls are on something?
- How many bowls are in the **n**?
- How many nails can you see?
- How many green bowls are there?
- How many blue bowls are there?
- How many boards make up the fence?
- How many spools of thread are in the picture?
- How many ties are polka dotted?
- How many are plain?
- How many are striped?

Memory and Phonemic Awareness

- Show illustrations **a** to **n**. Recite stories.
- Show cards **a** to **n**. Recite stories.
- Say letter names **a** to **n**. Recite letter stories.
- Say letter sounds **a** to **n**. Recite letter stories.
- Recite the letter stories, **a** to **n**, together, without cues.
- Ask the child to recite the letter stories, **a** to **n**, without cues. Prompt, if needed.

Ozzie Otter opens oysters

Alphabet Drill

If your child can recite the alphabet, by rote, go on to A-Z. If not, continue drilling for rote proficiency. (Many children are proficient by this point.)

Present the letter cards and recite the name of each letter along with your child as each letter card is presented. Repeat this exercise four or five times before moving on to the next segment in the lesson.

A-Z

Present the letter cards in order. Recite the names together as each card is presented. When you sense that your child is at the 95 percent proficiency level, conduct an individual checkout. The child names each of the letters as they appear. (The children who can recite the alphabet, by rote, usually carry the rote forward into this exercise.) If your child is proficient, do it once together before the individual checkout.

Z-A

If your child is proficient in A-Z, present the cards in reverse order Z-A. Recite the names together as each card is presented. If this is a new exercise, several repetitions are in order. If this is a relatively easy exercise for your child, do it once together before the individual checkout. Then move on to the next segment in the lesson.

Random Presentation for Developing Proficiency in Letter Name Recognition

If Z-A is proficient at the 95 percent level or better, take any source of print and have your child say the names of the letters as they appear in one or more sentences, or a paragraph. Read the sentences/paragraph aloud so your child can connect how letters form words, which combine to form sentences and paragraphs. Make a note of the speed of recognition. If it is slow, encourage faster recognition without inducing frustration. Increased speed of recognition follows naturally with increased familiarity with the letters.

Introduce Letter Story

- Introduce Ozzie Otter opens oysters.
- Drill to a level of functional recall.

Language Development and Visual Literacy

Check out the meanings of the words in the story and the vocabulary stimulated by the illustrations. Discuss your child's experiences with the animals and other aspects of the illustration.

- What is Ozzie holding in her hands?
- How can you tell that Ozzie likes oysters?
- What other animal do you see in the picture?
- In what bodies of water do we see large ships?
- What fruit do you see in the picture?
- Can you name the foods that are in the o?
- What is the white object we see on the oyster?
- Does Mom have pearls?
- How do pearls form in the oyster?
- The numbers that you see on the page are odd numbers.
- Why do we call an octopus an octopus?
- Where are the baby otters?
- Do you eat oysters?
- How do you cook them?
- What are ways in which to eat them?
- Do you like oysters?

Color

- What color is the oyster's shell?
- What color is the oyster?
- What color is the pearl?
- What color is the octopus?
- What are the two colors of the olives?
- What are the colors of the onions?
- True or false? An orange is purple?
- True or false? The ocean is blue?

Comprehension

- What is the story for o?
- What does Ozzie open?
- What kind of animal is Ozzie?
- What is the otter's name?
- What does the otter do?
- What does Ozzie Otter open?

Word Identification, Word Boundaries, Spelling

Word boundaries define where a word begins and ends. How many words are in the story? How many word boundaries are in the story? What are word boundaries?

- Which word is oysters? Spell it. What word did you spell?
- Which word is Otter? Spell it. What word did you spell?
- Which word is Ozzie? Spell it. What word did you spell?
- Which word is opens? Spell it. What word did you spell?

Ordinals

If this is a new exercise for your child, review the procedure established in the first few lessons. Use the current story to work up the concept.

If your child is familiar with ordinals, reduce the amount of time spent in review of the concept.

If your child is proficient, and you feel inclined to do so, ordinals cam be incorporated into the previous segment. Simply ask, "What is the fourth (last) word? Spell it. What word did you spell?"

- What is the fourth word?
- What is the second word?
- What is the first word?
- What is the third word?
- What is the last word?

Concepts

- Show me something that is close.
- Show me something that is far.
- Show me something that is round.
- Show me something that is oval.
- Show me two things in the o that are the same.
- Show me two things in the o that are different.
- Show me things that are pairs.
- Show me things that are floating on the water.

Counting and Estimating

- How many numbers are on the page?
- How many olives are on the page?
- How many green olives?
- How many green olives with pimiento?
- How many onions?
- How many otters?
- How many ships?
- How many oysters?
- How many whole oranges?
- How many parts of oranges?
- How many orange things on the page?
- How many blue things?
- How many round things?

Memory and Phonemic Awareness

- Show illustrations a to o Recite stories.
- Show cards a to o Recite stories.
- Say letter names a to o Recite stories.
- Say letter sounds a to o Recite stories.
- Recite the stories a to o together, without cues.
- Ask the child to recite the letter stories a to o without cues. Prompt, if needed.

Petie Penguin paints pictures

Alphabet Drill

If your child can recite the alphabet, by rote, go on to A-Z. If not, continue drilling for rote proficiency. (Many children are proficient by this point in the alphabet.)

Present the letter cards and recite the name of each letter along with your child as each letter card is presented. Repeat this exercise four or five times before moving on to the next segment in the lesson.

A-Z

Present the letter cards in order. Recite the names together as each card is presented. When you sense that your child is about 95 percent proficient, conduct an individual checkout. The child names each of the letters as they appear. (Children who can recite the alphabet by rote usually carry the rote forward into this exercise.) If your child is proficient, do it once together before the individual checkout.

Z-A

If your child is proficient in A-Z, present the cards in reverse order Z-A. Recite the names together as each card is presented. If this is a new exercise, several repetitions are in order. If this is a relatively easy exercise for your child, do it once together before the individual checkout. Then move on to the next segment in the lesson.

Random Presentation for Developing Proficiency in Letter Name Recognition

If Z-A is proficient at the 95 percent level, take any source of print and have your child say the names of the letters as they appear in one or more sentences, or a paragraph. Read the sentences/paragraph aloud so your child can connect how letters form words, which combine to form sentences and paragraphs. Make a note of the speed of recognition. If it is slow, encourage faster recognition without inducing frustration. Increased speed of recognition follows naturally with increased familiarity.

Introduce Letter Story

- Introduce Petie Penguin paints pictures.
- Drill to a functional level of recall.

Language Development and Visual Literacy

- Where do penguins live?
- Can penguins paint pictures?
- What do penguins eat?
- Show me pickles.
- Do you like pickles? Which are your favorite?
- Show me peanuts.
- Show me pumpkins.
- What do we do with pumpkins?
- When do we see lots of pumpkins?
- Show me paintings.
- Show me purple.
- Show me a paint brush.
- What is a tam? Is there one in the illustration? Show me.
- What is a palette? Who is holding one?
- Can penguins eat pickles?
- Do they eat peanuts?
- What is Petie standing on?
- Can pumpkins grow on an iceberg?
- What is an ice floe?
- How do pumpkins grow?

Color

- What color is a pumpkin?
- What color is the pickle?
- What color is the peanut?
- What color is the penguin?
- What color is the vine?
- What colors are in the iceberg?
- What color is the **p**?
- What color is the tam?

Comprehension

- What is the story for **p**?
- What kind of animal is in the story?
- What does the penguin do?
- What does the penguin paint?
- What is the penguin's name?
- Who paints pictures?

Word Identification, Word Boundaries, Spelling

Word boundaries define where a word begins and ends. How many words are in the story? How many word boundaries are in the story? What are word boundaries? How do we show them in writing?

- What is the second word? Spell it. What word did you spell?
- What is the third word? Spell it. What word did you spell?
- What is the fourth word? Spell it. What word did you spell?
- What is the first word? Spell it. What word did you spell?

Ordinals

If this is a new exercise for your child, review the procedure for this segment in the first few lessons. Use the current story to work up the concept.

If your child is relatively familiar with ordinals, shorten the review of the concept.

If your child is proficient, incorporate ordinals into Word Identification (as above), or work with it separately (as below).

- What is the second word?
- What is the third word?
- What is the fourth word?
- What is the first word?
- What is the last word?
- What are the two middle words?

Concepts

- Show me a penguin on a pumpkin.
- Show me penguins on the **p**.
- Show me penguins on an ice floe.
- Show me a penguin lying down.
- Show me a penguin standing up.
- Show me penguins sitting down.
- Show me a large penguin.
- Show me a small penguin.
- Show me a medium penguin.

- Show me a group of penguins.
- Shoe me a group of peanuts.
- Show me a painting of objects to eat.
- Show me a pair of pumpkins.
- Show me a pair of pickles.

Counting and Estimating

- How many penguins are on the page?
- How many pumpkins?
- How many peanuts?
- How many paintings?
- How many ice floes?
- How many pickles?
- How many paint brushes?
- How many leaves?
- Show me a group of two.
- Show me a group of three.
- Show me a pair.

Memory and Phonemic Awareness

- Show illustrations **a** to **p**. Recite stories.
- Show letter cards **a** to **p**. Recite stories.
- Say letter names **a** to **p**. Recite stories.
- Say letter sounds **a** to **p**. Recite stories.
- Recite stories **a** to **p**, together, without cues.
- Ask the child to recite the letter stories **a** to **p**, without cues. Prompt, if necessary.

Quilly Quail quivers quietly

Alphabet Drill

If your child can recite the alphabet, by rote, go on to A-Z. If not, continue drilling for rote proficiency. (Many children are proficient by this point in the alphabet. It is important to build in reinforcement practice at fairly regular intervals to ensure that the information moves from short-term memory to long-term memory. So, every fifth lesson, asking the child to recite the alphabet is most appropriate.) Present the letter cards and recite the name of each letter along with your child as each letter card is presented. Repeat this exercise four or five times before moving on to the next segment in the lesson.

A-Z

Present the letter cards in order. Recite the names together as each card is presented. When you sense that your child is about 95 percent proficient, conduct an individual checkout. The child names each of the letters as they appear. (Children who can recite the alphabet by rote usually carry the rote forward into this exercise. It is difficult to tell if the child is reading the cards or reciting by rote. That is why the reverse order Z-A is so very important. Z-A provides more conclusive proof that the child is reading the letter cards as presented.) If your child is proficient, do it once together before the individual checkout.

Z-A

If your child is proficient in A-Z, present the cards in reverse order Z-A. Recite the names together as each card is presented. If this is a new exercise, several repetitions are in order. If this is a relatively easy exercise for your child, do it once together before the individual checkout. Then move on to the next segment in the lesson.

Random Presentation for Developing Proficiency in Letter Name Recognition

If Z-A is proficient at the 95 percent level, take any source of print and have your child say the names of the letters as they appear in one or more sentences, or a paragraph. Read the sentences/paragraph aloud so your child can connect how letters form words, which combine to form sentences and paragraphs. Make a note of the speed of recognition. If it is slow, encourage faster recognition without inducing frustration. Increased speed of recognition follows naturally with increased familiarity with the alphabet.

Introduce Letter Story
- Introduce Quilly Quail quivers quietly.
- Drill to a functional level of recall.

Language Development and Visual Literacy

Discuss vocabulary arising from the illustrations and the story. Discuss the child's experiences with these elements.
- What is a quail? Have you ever seen one?
- What does quiver mean?
- What, in the illustration, shows that Quilly is quivering?
- What does quietly mean?
- What is the quail in the tree wearing?
- What kind of quail would she have to be if she were wearing a crown?
- Why do you suppose Quilly is quivering?
- What might she be afraid of?
- Point to the nest, asking, "What do we call this?"
- What is in the nest?
- What will happen to the eggs?
- What are those special marks beside the Queen Quail?
- What might the Queen be saying?
- Show me the quail family.
- What is a quilt?
- What is a patch?
- What are the objects in the patches on the quilt?

Color
- Tell me the colors of the quail.
- Describe the colors of the eggs.
- What colors are in the nest?
- What are the colors of the crown?
- What color are the leaves?
- What color is the **q**?

Comprehension
- What is the story for **q**?
- What does the animal in the story do?
- What kind of animal is it?
- How does the quail quiver?
- What is the quail's name?
- What does Quilly Quail do?

Word Identification, Word Boundaries, Spelling

Word boundaries define where a word begins and ends. How many words are in the story? How many word boundaries are in the story? What are word boundaries? What do they do? How do we show them in writing?

- What is the third word? Spell it. What word did you spell?
- What is the second word? Spell it. What word did you spell?
- What is the last word? Spell it. What word did you spell?
- What is the first word. Spell it. What word did you spell?

Ordinals

If this is a new exercise for your child, review the procedure for this segment in the first few lessons. Use the current story to work up the concept.

If your child is relatively familiar with ordinals, shorten the review of the concept.

If your child is gaining proficiency, incorporate ordinals into Word Identification (above) or work with it separately (below).

- What is the second word?
- What is the fourth word?
- What is the first word?
- What is the third word?
- What is the last word?
- What are the two middle words in the sentence?

Concepts

- Point to a quail at the top of the page.
- Point to a quail at the bottom of the page.
- Point to a quail on the right.
- Point to a quail on the left.
- Show me eggs in the nest.
- Show me eggs out of the nest.
- Point to an egg in the **q**.
- Point to an egg out of the **q**.
- Show me a question mark at the top of the page.
- Show me a quail in the tree.

- Show me a quail out of the tree.
- What is on the quail in the tree?
- Show me an egg in the quilt.
- Show me an egg out of the quilt.
- Name one of the objects in the patches.
- What is the opposite of quiet?

Counting and Estimating

- How many quail are on the page?
- How many eggs are in the nest?
- How many dark blue eggs are in the **q**?
- How many light blue eggs are in the **q**?
- How many grey eggs are in the **q**?
- Remove picture plate. Ask, "About how many eggs are in the **q**?"
- How many quail are in the family?
- How many patches can you see on the quilt?
- How many question marks can you see?

Memory and Phonemic Awareness

- Show illustrations **a** to **q**. Recite stories.
- Show letter cards **a** to **q**. Recite stories.
- Say letter names **a** to **q**. Recite stories.
- Say letter sounds **a** to **q**. Recite stories.
- Recite stories **a** to **q**, together, without cues.
- Ask the child to recite the letter stories **a** to **q**, without cues. Prompt, if necessary.

Robbie Rhino runs races

Alphabet Drill

If your child can recite the alphabet, by rote, go on to A-Z. Do remember to build in reinforcement practice, at regular intervals, to ensure movement from short-term to long-term memory. If not, continue drilling for rote proficiency.

A-Z

Present the letter cards in order. Recite the names together as each card is presented. If your child is proficient, complete an individual checkout. Children who can recite the alphabet by rote usually carry the rote forward into this exercise. It is difficult to tell if the child is "reading" the cards or reciting by rote. Z-A provides more conclusive proof that the child is reading the letter cards as presented. If your child is proficient, do it once together before the individual checkout. If not, continue drilling for proficiency.

Z-A

If your child is proficient in A-Z, present the cards in reverse order Z-A. Recite the names together as each card is presented. If this is a new exercise, repeat the series several times. If this is an easy exercise for your child, do it once together, run an individual checkout, and move on to the next segment in the lesson.

Random Presentation for Developing Proficiency in Letter Name Recognition

If Z-A is proficient, take any source of print and have your child say the names of the letters as they appear in one or more sentences, or a paragraph. Read the sentences/paragraph aloud so your child can connect how letters form words, which combine to form sentences and paragraphs. Make a note of the speed of recognition. If it is labored, encourage faster recognition without inducing frustration. Increased speed of recognition follows naturally with increased familiarity with the alphabet.

Introduce Letter Story
- Introduce Robbie Rhino runs races.
- Drill to a functional level of recall.

Language Development and Visual Literacy

Discuss vocabulary concepts arising from the illustrations and the story. Discuss your child's experiences with these elements.
- What is a rhino? What is it short for?
- In the race, who came in first?
- What color ribbon is she wearing?
- What does a blue ribbon mean?
- Who came in second?
- What color ribbon would the rat get?
- Who came in third?
- What color ribbon would the rabbit get?
- What does a red ribbon mean?
- What does a white ribbon mean?
- What do we call the special place where races are held?
- Point to the lanes. Ask, What do these lines mean?"
- Who looks happy?
- Who looks really tired?
- Who looks surprised and disappointed?
- Who thinks he should have won the race?
- Do animals really run races?
- What are the objects in the **r**?
- What is Robbie wearing?

Color
- What color is the **r**?
- What color is the track?
- What color is the rabbit?
- Is a real rabbit yellow?
- What color is the mouse? When is a mouse that color?
- Show me the white running shoe.
- Show me a red running shoe.
- What color is the ribbon that Robbie ran into when he won the race?

Comprehension
- What is the story for **r**?
- What does the animal do?
- What is the animal's name?
- What kind of animal is it?
- What does Robbie Rhino do?
- What does the Rhino run?

Word Identification, Word Boundaries, Spelling

Word boundaries define where a word begins and ends. How many words are in the story? How many word boundaries are in the story? What are word boundaries? What do they do? How do we show word boundaries in writing?

- What is the third word? Spell it. What word did you spell?
- What is the fourth word? Spell it. What word did you spell?
- What is the first word? Spell it. What word did you spell?
- What is the second word? Spell it. What word did you spell?

Ordinals

If this is a new exercise for your child, review the procedure for this segment in the early lessons. Use the current story to work up the concept.

If your child is familiar with the ordinals, shorten the review. If your child is proficient, incorporate ordinals into Word Identification (above) or drill separately (below).

- What is the third word?
- What is the fourth word?
- What is the last word?
- What is the first word?
- What is the second word?
- Going from the top of the **r** to the bottom, point to each shoe while stating its order.
- Going from bottom to top in the **r**, point to each shoe while stating its order.
- What are the two middle words in the sentence?

Concepts
- Point to the blue ribbon on the left.
- What place is it?
- Point to the white ribbon on the right.
- What place is it?
- Point to the red ribbon in the centre.
- What place is it?
- Point to the shoe at the top of the **r**.
- Point to the shoe at the bottom of the **r**.
- Point to the shoe at the bottom of the page.
- Look at the **r**. Two shoes point to the left. Which ones are they?
- One shoe is pointing to the top of the **r**. Which one is it?
- One shoe is pointing to the right. Which one is it?
- Show me an animal's foot that is up.
- Show me an animal's foot that is down.

Counting and Estimating
- How many animals are on the page?
- How many shoes are on the page?
- How many words are on the page?
- How many ribbons are on the page?

Memory and Phonemic Awareness
- Show illustrations **a** to **r**. Recite stories.
- Show letter cards **a** to **r**. Recite stories.
- Say letter names **a** to **r**. Recite stories.
- Say letter sounds **a** to **r**. Recite stories.
- Recite stories **a** to **r**, together, without cues.
- Ask the child to recite the letter stories **a** to **r**, without cues, prompting if and where necessary.

Suzie Seal sings songs

Alphabet Drill

If your child can recite the alphabet, by rote, go on to A-Z. Remember to build in reinforcement practice, at regular intervals, to ensure movement from short-term to long-term memory. If not, continue drilling for rote recitation.

A-Z

Present the letter cards, in order. Recite the names together as each card is presented. If your child is proficient, complete an individual checkout. Children who can recite the alphabet by rote usually carry the rote forward into this exercise. It is difficult to tell if the child is "reading" the cards or reciting by rote. Z-A provides more conclusive proof that the child is reading the letter cards as presented. If your child is proficient, do it once together before the individual checkout. If not, continue drilling for proficiency.

Z-A

If your child is proficient in A-Z, present the cards in reverse order Z-A. Recite the names together as each card is presented. If this is a new exercise, repeat the series several times. If this is an easy exercise for your child, do it once together, run an individual checkout, and move on to the next segment in the lesson.

Random Presentation for Developing Proficiency in Letter Name Recognition

If Z-A is proficient, take any source of print and have your child say the names of the letters as they appear in one or more sentences, or a paragraph. Read the sentences/paragraph aloud so your child can connect how letters form words, which combine to form sentences and paragraphs. Make a note of the speed of recognition. If it is slow, encourage faster recognition without inducing frustration. Increased speed of recognition follows naturally with increased familiarity with the alphabet.

Introduce Letter Story
- Introduce Suzie Seal sings songs.
- Drill for functional recall.

Language Development and Visual Literacy

Discuss vocabulary concepts arising from the illustrations and the story. Discuss your child's experiences with these elements.
- Show me a seal.
- Have you seen a real seal? Where?
- Where do many seals live?
- What do they eat?
- Can seals sing?
- What kinds of shells are on the sand?
- Where is the snail?
- Can you find the sand dollar?
- Which shell is the scallop?
- Which one is the conch?
- What images are in the **s**?
- True or false. The sun is sad?
- Why is the sun happy?
- What is the seal sitting on?
- What is the seal wearing?
- What is that in Suzie's flipper?
- What does a microphone do?

Color
- Show me a pink shell.
- Show me a brown shell.
- What color is the **s**?
- Name the colors of the stars starting at the top of the **s**.
- What color is the seal?
- What color is the scarf?
- What color is the sun?

Comprehension
- What is the story for **s**?
- What is the seal's name?
- What kind of animal is Suzie?
- What does Suzie sing?
- What does Suzie do?
- Who sings songs?
- Why does Suzie sing songs?

Word Identification, Word Boundaries, Spelling

Word boundaries define where a word begins and ends. How many words are in the story? How many word boundaries are in the story? What are word boundaries? What do they do? How do we show word boundaries in writing?

- What is the first word? Spell it. What word did you spell?
- What is the second word? Spell it. What word did you spell?
- What is the fourth word? Spell it. What word did you spell?
- What is the third word? Spell it. What word did you spell?
- What is the last word? Spell it. What word did you spell?

Ordinals

If this is a new exercise for your child, review the procedure for this segment in the early lessons. Use the current story to work up the concept.

If your child is familiar with the ordinals, shorten the review.

If your child is proficient, incorporate ordinals into Word Identification (above) or drill separately (below).

- Tell me the first word.
- Tell me the second word.
- Tell me the fourth word.
- Tell me the third word.
- Tell me the two middle words.
- Tell me the two end words.

Concepts

- Point to an animal on the rocks.
- Point to an animal on the sand.
- Point to the shell on the left.
- Point to the shell on the right.
- Point to the object in Suzie's hand.
- Point to the animal whose body is half out of the shell.
- Where is the musical staff?

Counting and Estimating

- How many shells are on the beach?
- How many big rocks can you see?
- How many seals are in the picture?
- How many green stars are in the picture?
- How many yellow stars are in the picture?
- How many notes are on the staff?
- How many seals are singing?

Memory and Phonemic Awareness

- Show illustrations **a** to **s**. Recite stories.
- Show letter cards **a** to **s**. Recite stories.
- Say letter names **a** to **s**. Recite stories.
- Say letter sounds **a** to **s**. Recite stories.
- Recite stories **a** to **s**, together, without cues.
- Ask the child to recite the letter stories **a** to **s**, without cues, prompting when necessary.

Tommy Tiger tells time

Alphabet Drill

If your child can recite the alphabet, by rote, go on to A-Z. Remember to build in reinforcement practice, at regular intervals, to ensure movement from short-term to long-term memory. If not, continue drilling for rote recitation.

A-Z

Present the letter cards, in order. Recite the names together as each card is presented. If your child is proficient, complete an individual checkout. Children who can recite the alphabet by rote usually carry the rote forward into this exercise. It is difficult to tell if the child is "reading" the letter cards or reciting by rote. Z-A provides more conclusive proof that the child is reading the letter cards, as presented. If your child is proficient, do it once together before the individual checkout. If not, continue drilling for proficiency.

Z-A

If your child is proficient in A-Z, present the cards in reverse order Z-A. Recite the names together as each card is presented. If this is a new exercise, repeat the series several times. If this is an easy exercise for your child, do it once together, run an individual checkout, and move on to the next segment in the lesson.

Random Presentation for Developing Proficiency in Letter Name Recognition

If Z-A is proficient, take any source of print and have your child say the names of the letters as they appear in one or more sentences, or a paragraph. Read the sentences/paragraph aloud so your child can connect how letters form words, which combine to form sentences and paragraphs. Make a note of speed of recognition. If it is slow, encourage faster recognition without inducing frustration. Increased speed of recognition follows quite naturally with increased familiarity with the alphabet.

Introduce Letter Story
- Introduce Tommy Tiger tells time.
- Drill to a functional level of recall.

Language Development and Visual Literacy

Discuss vocabulary concepts arising from the illustrations and the story. Discuss your child's experiences with these elements.
- What is Tommy pointing to?
- What is he holding in one hand?
- What is he holding in the other hand?
- What is Tommy wearing?
- What kind of clocks are on the table?
- What kind of clock is hanging on the wall?
- What is that big clock called?
- Why is it called that?
- What is in the t?
- What kind of animal is Tommy?

Color
- Show me the pink, digital clock.
- Show me the yellow stopwatch.
- Show me the brown cuckoo clock.
- Show me the red, alarm clock.
- Show me the big, brown clock.
- What color is the t?
- What color is the toothbrush with toothpaste on it?
- What color is the other toothbrush?
- What color is Tommy's hat?
- What color is Tommy?

Comprehension
- What is the story for t?
- What kind of animal is in the story?
- What does the Tiger tell?
- What does the Tiger do?
- What is the name of the Tiger?
- Who tells time?
- What does Tommy Tiger do?
- Do you know how to tell time?

Word Identification, Word Boundaries, Spelling

- How many words are in the story? How many word boundaries are in the story?
- How do we show word boundaries in writing?
- What is the second word? Spell it. What word did you spell?
- What is the fourth word? Spell it. What word did you spell?
- What is the third word? Spell it. What word did you spell?
- What is the first word? Spell it. What word did you spell?
- What is the last word? Spell it. What word did you spell?

Ordinals

If this is a new exercise for your child, review the procedure for this segment in the early lessons. Use the current story to develop the concept.

If your child is familiar with ordinals, shorten the review.

If your child is proficient, incorporate ordinals into Word Identification (above) or drill separately (below).
- Tell me the second word.
- Tell me the fourth word.
- Point to the third word.
- Show me the first word.
- Which word is tells? Is it the first, second, third, or fourth word?
- Which word is Tommy? Is it the first, second, third, or fourth word?
- Which word is Tiger? Is it the first, second, third, or fourth word?
- Which word is time? Is it the first, second, third, or fourth word?
- Which words are the two middle words?
- Which are the two end words?

Concepts

- Is the **t** on the left or on the right?
- Is Tommy sitting down or standing up?
- Is Tommy pointing up or pointing down?
- What is the tall thing on the left?
- What kind of clock is above Tommy's head?
- Point to the clocks below Tommy's arm.
- What are those clocks sitting on?
- Is the tube of toothpaste at the top of the **t** or at the bottom?
- Point to the toothbrush at the top.
- Point to the toothbrush that has toothpaste on it.

Counting and Estimating

- How many clocks are on the page?
- How many toothbrushes are on the page?
- How many clocks have round dials?
- How many clocks make a ringing sound?
- How many items are in the **t**? (Remove the picture before asking.)

Memory and Phonemic Awareness

- Show illustrations **a** to **t**. Recite stories.
- Show letter cards **a** to **t**. Recite stories.
- Say letter names **a** to **t**. Recite stories.
- Say letter sounds **a** to **t**. Recite stories.
- Recite stories **a** to **t**, together, without cues.
- Ask the child to recite the letter stories **a** to **t**, without cues, prompting if and when necessary.

Uncle Unicorn uses ukuleles

Alphabet Drill

If your child can recite the alphabet, by rote, go on to A-Z. Remember to build in reinforcement practice, at regular intervals, to ensure movement from short-term to long-term memory. If not, continue drilling for rote recitation.

A-Z

Present the letter cards, in order. Recite the names together as each card is presented. If your child is proficient, complete an individual checkout. Children who can recite the alphabet, by rote, usually carry that forward into this exercise. If is difficult, therefore, to tell if the child is "reading" the cards or reciting by rote. Z-A provides more conclusive proof that the child is "reading" the letter cards, as presented. If your child is proficient, do it once together before the individual checkout. If not, continue drilling for proficiency.

Z-A

If your child is proficient in A-Z, present the cards in reverse order Z-A. Recite the names together as each card is presented. If this is a new exercise, repeat the series several times. If this is an easy exercise for your child, do it once together, run an individual checkout, and move on to the next segment in the lesson.

Random Presentation for Developing Proficiency in Letter Name Recognition

If Z-A is proficient, take any source of print and have your child say the names of the letters as they appear in one or more sentences, or a paragraph. Read the sentences/paragraph aloud so your child can connect how letters form words, which combine to form sentences and paragraphs. Make a note of speed of recognition. If it is slow, encourage faster recognition without inducing frustration. Increased speed of recognition follows quite naturally with increased familiarity with the alphabet.

Introduce Letter Story
- Introduce Uncle Unicorn uses ukuleles.
- Drill to a functional level of recall.

Language Development and Visual Literacy

Discuss vocabulary concepts arising from the illustrations and the story. Discuss your child's experiences with these elements.
- What do you think a ukulele is?
- What are spurs?
- What kind of boots is Uncle Unicorn wearing?
- Is a unicorn a real or imaginary animal?
- How do you know?
- How do you play a ukulele?
- What are the objects in the **u**?
- What do we call the green plant in the picture?

Color
- What color is the **u**?
- Name the colors of the umbrellas in the **u**.
- What color is the plant?
- What is the color of the umbrella on the plant?
- What color is the Unicorn's tail and mane?
- What color are his boots?
- What color are the spurs?
- Show me a brown umbrella.
- What color is the Unicorn's vest?

Comprehension
- What is the story for **u**?
- What is the name of the musical instrument?
- What kind of animal is in the story?
- What does he do?
- What is the Unicorn's name?
- Who uses ukuleles?
- What does Uncle Unicorn do?

Word Identification, Word Boundaries, Spelling

What is a word boundary? How many of them are in the story? How do we show word boundaries in writing?
- What is the fourth word? Spell it. What word did you spell?
- What is the second word? Spell it. What word did you spell?
- What is the third word? Spell it. What word did you spell?
- What is the first word? Spell it. What word did you spell?
- What is the last word? Spell it. What word did you spell?

Ordinals

If this is a new exercise for your child, review the procedure for this segment in the early lessons. Use the current story to develop the concept.

If your child is familiar with ordinals, shorten the review.

If your child is proficient, incorporate ordinals into Word Identification (above) or drill separately (below).
- Show me the fourth word.
- Show me the second word.
- Show me the third word.
- Show me the first word.
- What are the two middle words?
- Which are the two end words?
- Which word is uses? Is it the first, second, third, or fourth word?
- Which word is ukulele?
- Which word is Unicorn?
- Which word is Uncle?

Concepts
- Show me an umbrella that is closed.
- Show me an umbrella that is opened.
- Show me an umbrella that is upside down.
- Show me an umbrella that is right side up.
- Show me an umbrella that leans to the right.
- Show me an umbrella that leans to the left.
- Show me an umbrella on the cactus.
- Show me an umbrella under the cactus.

Counting and Estimating
- How many unicorns are on the page?
- How many ukuleles?
- How many umbrellas are on the page?
- About how many umbrellas are in the **u**? Remove the page before you ask the question.

Memory and Phonemic Awareness
- Show illustrations **a** to **u**. Recite stories.
- Show letter cards **a** to **u**. Recite stories.
- Say letter names **a** to **u**. Recite stories.
- Say letter sounds **a** to **u**. Recite stories.
- Recite stories **a** to **u**, together, without cues.
- Ask the child to recite the letter stories **a** to **u**, without cues, prompting if and when necessary.

Vinnie Vulture views valentines

Alphabet Drill

If your child can recite the alphabet, by rote, go on to A-Z. Remember to build in reinforcement practice, at regular intervals, to ensure movement from short-term to long-term memory. If not, continue drilling for rote recitation.

A-Z

Present the letter cards, in order. Recite the names together as each card is presented. If your child is proficient, complete an individual checkout. Children who can recite the alphabet, by rote, usually carry that forward into this exercise. It is difficult, therefore, to tell if the child is "reading" the cards or reciting by rote. Z-A provides more conclusive proof that the child is "reading" the letter cards, as presented. If your child is proficient, do it once together before the individual checkout. If not, continue drilling for proficiency.

Z-A

If your child is proficient, take any source of print and have your child say the names of the letters as they appear in one or more sentences, or a paragraph. Read the sentences/paragraph aloud so your child can connect how letters form words, which combine to form sentences and paragraphs. Make a note of speed of recognition. If it is slow, encourage faster recognition without inducing frustration. Increased speed of recognition follows quite naturally with increased familiarity with the alphabet.

Introduce Letter Story

- Introduce Vinnie Vulture views valentines.
- Drill to a functional level of recall.

Language Development and Visual Literacy

Discuss vocabulary concepts arising from the illustrations and the story. Discuss your child's experiences with these elements.

- Tell me what you recognize in the picture.
- What kind of bird is it?
- What happened to the mountain?
- What is hanging on the vine?
- What do we call the things that are in the **v**?

After the child has named the items individually, ask what we call this class of food. What is the collective noun for these items?

- Ask the child to read the valentines.
- Draw attention to the names of the animals used in the stories if the child doesn't notice. Some will recognize them immediately, others will have to be led to the conclusion.
- What is a vulture? What does a vulture eat?

The chain of mountains along the West Coast include active volcanoes in Mount Baker, Mount Rainier, Mount St. Helen's, and Mount Shasta. What happened to Mount St. Helen's?

- What does view mean?

Color

- What color is the **v**?
- What color are the valentines?
- What color is the volcano?
- What color is the Vulture?
- Name the color of each of the vegetables.

Comprehension

- What is the story for **v**?
- What is the animal's name?
- What does Vinnie do?
- What does Vinnie visit?
- What is Vinnie?
- Who views valentines?

Word Identification, Word Boundaries, Spelling

- How do we show word boundaries in writing? How many word boundaries are in this story?
- What is the first word? Spell it. What word did you spell?
- What is the third word? Spell it. What word did you spell?
- What is the fourth word? Spell it. What word did you spell?
- What is the second word? Spell it. What word did you spell?

Ordinals

- Show me the fourth word.
- Show me the third word.
- Show me the second word.
- Show me the first word.
- Vulture. Which word is it? First, second, third, or last?
- Vinnie. Which word is it?
- Valentines. Which word is it?
- Views. Which word is it?
- Which are the two middle words?
- Which are the two end words?

Concepts

- Which vegetable is below the carrot?
- Which vegetable is above the beet?
- Which vegetable is below the rutabaga?
- Which vegetable is above the potato?
- Which two vegetables are above the peapod?
- Is the volcano above or below the vulture?
- Which valentine is at the top?
- Which valentine is at the bottom?
- Where is the **v**? On the left or on the right?
- Which valentine is between Annie and Leo and Harley and Eadie?

Counting and Estimating

- How many valentines are on the page?
- How many vegetables are in the **v**?

Memory and Phonemic Awareness

- Show illustrations A to **v**. Recite stories.
- Show letter cards A to **v**. Recite stories.
- Say letter names A to **v**. Recite stories.
- Say letter sounds A to **v**. Recite stories.
- Recite stories A to **v**, together, without cues.
- Ask the child to recite the letter stories A to **v**, without cues, prompting if and when necessary.

Wally Wolf washes wigs

Alphabet Drill

If your child can recite the alphabet, by rote, go on to A-Z. Remember to build in reinforcement practice, at regular intervals, to ensure movement from short-term to long-term memory. If not, continue drilling for rote recitation.

A-Z

Present the letter cards, in order. Recite the names together as each card is presented. If your child is proficient, complete an individual checkout. Children who can recite the alphabet, by rote, usually carry that forward into this exercise. It is difficult, therefore, to tell if the child is 'reading' the cards or reciting by rote. Z-A provides more conclusive proof that the child is 'reading' the letter cards, as presented. If your child is proficient, do it once together before the individual checkout. If not, continue drilling for proficiency.

Z-A

If your child is proficient, take any source of print and have your child say the names of the letters as they appear in one or more sentences, or a paragraph. Read the sentences/paragraph aloud so your child can connect how letters form words, which combine to form sentences and paragraphs. Make a note of speed of recognition. If it is slow, encourage faster recognition without inducing frustration. Increased speed of recognition follows quite naturally with increased familiarity with the alphabet.

Introduce Letter Story

- Introduce Wally Wolf washes wigs.
- Drill to a functional level of recall.

Language Development and Visual Literacy

Discuss vocabulary concepts arising from the illustrations and the story. Discuss your child's experiences with these elements.
- What is a wig?
- Who would wear one? Why?
- What is Wally wearing?
- What is he washing?
- What is coming out of the wig?
- What does he use to hang the wigs on the line?
- What insect is in the **w**?
- What food is in the **w**?
- Is the wig Wally is holding wet or dry? How do you know?
- What is Wally wearing on his arm?
- What are the poles for the clothesline made of?
- What does Wally wash the wigs in?
- Show me the whole walnuts.

Color

- What color is the wig Wally is wearing? (Blonde)
- What color is the wig he is holding? (Brown)
- What color is the first wig hanging on the line? (Dark blonde)
- What color is the next wig? (Red)
- What color is the last wig? (Sandy brown)
- What color are Wally's pants?
- What color is the **w**?
- What color are the worms?
- What color is the washtub?

Comprehension

- What is the story for **w**?
- What is the animal washing?
- What is the animal's name?
- What is the animal doing?
- What kind of animal is in the story?
- What does Wally Wolf do?
- What does he wash?

Word Identification, Word Boundaries, Spelling

- How do we show word boundaries in writing? How many word boundaries are in the story?
- What is the fourth word? Spell it. What word did you spell?
- What is the first word? Spell it. What word did you spell?
- What is the third word? Spell it. What word did you spell?
- What is the second word? Spell it. What word did you spell?

Ordinals

- Show me the fourth word.
- Show me the first word.
- Show me the third word.
- Show me the second word.
- Which word is wigs? First, second, third, or fourth?
- Which word is Wally?
- Which word is washes?
- Which word is Wolf?
- What are the two middle words?
- What are the two end words?

Concepts

- Show me a curly wig. Show me a straight wig.
- Point to the wig that Wally is wearing.
- Point to the whole walnuts.
- Point to the half walnuts.
- Point to the wig in Wally's hands.
- Point to the wigs that are on the line.
- Show me a wig that is wet. Show me one that looks dry.

Counting and Estimating

- How many wigs are wet?
- How many wigs appear dry?
- How many walnuts are whole?
- How many worms are there?
- How many half walnuts are in the **w**?
- How many wigs are on the page?
- How many poles are there?
- Remove the page from sight and ask, "About how many objects are in the **w**?"

Memory and Phonemic Awareness

- Show illustrations **a** to **w**. Recite stories.
- Show letter cards **a** to **w**. Recite stories.
- Say letter names **a** to **w**. Recite stories.
- Say letter sounds **a** to **w**. Recite stories.
- Recite stories **a** to **w**, together, without cues.
- Ask the child to recite the letter stories, **a** to **w**, without cues. Prompt if and when necessary.

X marks it wrong

Alphabet Drill

If your child can recite the alphabet, by rote, go on to A-Z. Remember to build in reinforcement practice, at regular intervals, to ensure movement from short-term to long-term memory. If not, continue drilling for rote recitation.

A-Z

Present the letter cards, in order. Recite the names together as each card is presented. If your child is proficient, complete an individual checkout. Children who can recite the alphabet, by rote, usually carry that forward into this exercise. It is difficult, therefore, to tell if the child is 'reading' the cards or reciting by rote. Z-A provides more conclusive proof that the child is 'reading' the letter cards, as presented. If your child is proficient, do it once together before the individual checkout. If not, continue drilling for proficiency.

Z-A

If your child is proficient, take any source of print and have your child say the names of the letters as they appear in one or more sentences, or a paragraph. Read the sentences/paragraph aloud so your child can connect how letters form words, which combine to form sentences and paragraphs. Make a note of speed of recognition. If it is slow, encourage faster recognition without inducing frustration. Increased speed of recognition follows quite naturally with increased familiarity with the alphabet.

Introduce Letter Story

- Introduce X marks it wrong.
- Drill to a functional level of recall.

Language Development and Visual Literacy

Discuss vocabulary concepts arising from the illustrations and the story. Discuss your child's experiences with these elements.

- Do you see all the objects with the **x** on them?
- What does it mean?
- What room of a house are we seeing?
- What do you see through the window? (A cross-walk signal)
- What does the hand mean?
- What is on the window sill?
- Why is the **x** on them.
- What is on the stove?
- How do you know that the kettle is very hot?
- Look at the tap on the sink. Is that hot water or cold water coming out of the tap?
- What is sticking out of the drawer?
- What is under the sink? (Dangerous chemicals in the cleaners.)
- What does the skull and crossbones mean?
- What is dangerous about wall sockets?
- Look at the halogen lamp. It burns extremely hot. Anything placed near it could burn.
- What kind of dog is in the picture?
- What is he looking at?
- Discuss the training and utility of guide dogs.

Color

- What color are the curtains?
- What color is the **x**?
- What color is the dog?
- What color is the stove?
- What color are the clouds?

Comprehension

- What is the story for **x**?
- What marks it wrong?
- What does **x** do?

Word Identification, Word Boundaries, Spelling
- What is the third word? Spell it. What word did you spell?
- What is the fourth word? Spell it. What word did you spell?
- What is the second word? Spell it. What word did you spell?

Ordinals
- Show me the word "it." What is its ordinal position?
- Show me the **x**. What is its ordinal position?
- Show me the word wrong. What is its ordinal position?
- Show me the word marks. What is its ordinal position?

Concepts
- Show me an open drawer. Show me one that is closed.
- Show me a pill bottle that is opened. Show me one that is closed.
- Show me a pill bottle that is upright. Show me one that is on its side.
- Show me a large pill bottle. Show me a small pill bottle. Show me one that is neither large nor small.
- Show me the object that you see through the window.
- Show me a cabinet door that is open. Show me one that is closed.
- Look at the pill bottle that is opened. Show me the pills in the bottle. Show me the pills out of the bottle.

Counting and Estimating
- How many **x**'s are on the page?
- Count the kettles. How many are there?
- How many wall sockets, pill bottles, knives, chemical containers, drawers, cabinet doors, sinks, torchere lamps, dogs, stoves, curtains, and windows… are there?

Memory and Phonemic Awareness
- Show illustrations **a** to **x**. Recite stories.
- Show letter cards **a** to **x**. Recite stories.
- Say letter names **a** to **x**. Recite stories.
- Say letter sounds **a** to **x**. Recite stories.]
- Recite stories **a** to **x**, together, without cues.
- Ask the child to recite the letter stories **a** to **x**, without cues, prompting if and when necessary.

Yonita Yak yodels yes

Alphabet Drill

If your child can recite the alphabet, by rote, go on to A-Z. Remember to build in reinforcement practice, at regular intervals, to ensure movement from short-term to long-term memory. If not, continue drilling for rote recitation.

A-Z

Present the letter cards, in order. Recite the names together as each card is presented. If your child is proficient, complete an individual checkout. Children who can recite the alphabet, by rote, usually carry that forward into this exercise. It is difficult, therefore, to tell if the child is 'reading' the cards or reciting by rote. Z-A provides more conclusive proof that the child is 'reading' the letter cards, as presented. If your child is proficient, do it once together before the individual checkout. If not, continue drilling for proficiency.

Z-A

If your child is proficient, take any source of print and have your child say the names of the letters as they appear in one or more sentences, or a paragraph. Read the sentences/paragraph aloud so your child can connect how letters form words, which combine to form sentences and paragraphs. Make a note of speed of recognition. If it is slow, encourage faster recognition without inducing frustration. Increased speed of recognition usually follows increased familiarity with the alphabet.

Introduce Letter Story

- Introduce Yonita Yak yodels yes.
- Drill to a functional level of recall.

Language Development and Visual Literacy

Discuss vocabulary concepts arising from the illustrations and the story. Discuss your child's experiences with these elements.

- What is a Yak? Where do they live?
- What is the Yak saying?
- Why is she saying Yes?
- What is in the **y**?
- What do you do with yarn?
- What does yodels mean? What do you do when you yodel?
- Which nation is famous for yodeling?
- What else is in the **y**?
- What do you do with a yo-yo?
- What is in the water?
- What is the bird on the **y** holding in its beak?
- Where is the Yak standing?

Color

- What color is the Yak?
- What color is the water?
- What color is the bird?
- What are the colors of the yarn?
- What are the colors of the yo-yos?
- What is the color of the **y**?
- What is the color of the yachts?

Comprehension

- What is the story for **y**?
- What kind of animal is in the story?
- What does the Yak yodel?
- What is the Yak's name?
- What does the Yak do?
- Who yodels yes?
- What does Yonita Yak do?

Word Identification, Word Boundaries, Spelling
- What is the second word? Spell it. What word did you spell?
- What is the fourth word? Spell it. What word did you spell?
- What is the first word? Spell it. What word did you spell?
- What is the third word? Spell it. What word did you spell?

Ordinals
- Show me the word Yak. What is its ordinal position?
- Show me the word yes. What is its ordinal position?
- Show me the word Yonita. What is its ordinal position?
- Show me the word yodels. What is its ordinal position?

Concepts
- Is Yonita standing above the clouds or below the clouds?
- What else is below Yonita? (Yachts, ocean)
- Does Yonita have her head up or down?
- Show me the yacht that is sailing left… that is sailing right.

Counting and Estimating
- How many balls of yarn are in the picture?
- How many yo-yos? How many yachts?
- How many clouds?
- How many **y**'s.

Memory and Phonemic Awareness
- Show illustrations **a** to **y**. Recite stories.
- Show letter cards **a** to **y**. Recite stories.
- Say letter names **a** to **y**. Recite stories.
- Say letter sounds **a** to **y**. Recite stories.
- Recite stories **a** to **y**, together, without cues.
- Ask the child to recite the letter stories, **a** to **y**, without cues.

Zeke Zebra zings zithers

Alphabet Drill

If your child can recite the alphabet, by rote, go on to A-Z. Remember to build in reinforcement practice, at regular intervals, to ensure movement from short-term to long-term memory. If not, continue drilling for rote recitation.

A-Z

Present the letter cards, in order. Recite the names together as each card is presented. If your child is proficient, complete an individual checkout. Children who can recite the alphabet, by rote, usually carry that forward into this exercise. It is difficult, therefore, to tell If the child is 'reading' the cards or reciting by rote. Z-A provides more conclusive proof that the child is 'reading' the letter cards, as presented. If your child is proficient, do it once together before the individual checkout. If not, continue drilling for proficiency.

Z-A

If your child is proficient, take any source of print and have your child say the names of the letters as they appear in one or more sentences, or a paragraph. Read the sentences/paragraph aloud so your child can connect how letters form words, which combine to form sentences and paragraphs. Make a note of speed of recognition. If it is slow, encourage faster recognition without inducing frustration. Increased speed of recognition usually follows increased familiarity with the alphabet.

Introduce Letter Story

- Introduce Zeke Zebra zings zithers.
- Drill to a functional level of recall.

Language Development and Visual Literacy

Discuss vocabulary concepts arising from the illustrations and the story. Discuss your child's experiences with these elements.
- Have you ever seen a zebra? Where?
- What is the zebra holding?
- What is a zither?
- How do you play it?
- What does zing mean?
- What is in the sky?
- What does a zeppelin do?
- What is happening at the zoo?
- What is in the **z**?
- What does a zipper do?

Color

- What color is the zebra?
- What color is the zeppelin?
- What color is the zither?
- What color are the zippers?
- What color is the rabbit?
- What color is the rhinoceros?

Comprehension

- What is the story for **z**?
- What kind of animal is in the story?
- What is the animal's name?
- What does the zebra do?
- What does the zebra zing?

Word Identification, Word Boundaries, Spelling

- What is the second word? Spell it. What word did you spell?
- What is the first word? Spell it. What word did you spell?
- What is the third word? Spell it. What word did you spell?
- What is the fourth word? Spell it. What word did you spell?

Ordinals
- Zebra. What is its ordinal position in the sentence?
- Zeke. What is its ordinal position in the sentence?
- Zings. What is its ordinal position in the sentence?
- Zithers. What is its ordinal position in the sentence?

Concepts
- Show me part of a zipper that is open… that is closed.
- Is the gate to the zoo open or closed?
- Is the ladder from the zeppelin hanging up or hanging down?
- Is the zebra standing or sitting?
- Is the rabbit running toward the gate or away from the gate?

Counting and Estimating
- How many animals are in the picture?
- How many zippers are there?
- How many vehicles are in the picture?
- How many notes has the zebra sung?
- How many parts to the gate are there?

Memory and Phonemic Awareness
- Show illustrations **a** to **z**. Recite stories.
- Show letter cards **a** to **z**. Recite stories.
- Say letter names **a** to **z**. Recite stories.
- Say letter sounds **a** to **z**. Recite stories.
- Recite stories **a** to **z**, together, without cues.
- Ask the child to recite the letter stories, **a** to **z**, without cues. Prompt if and when necessary.

Letter Cards

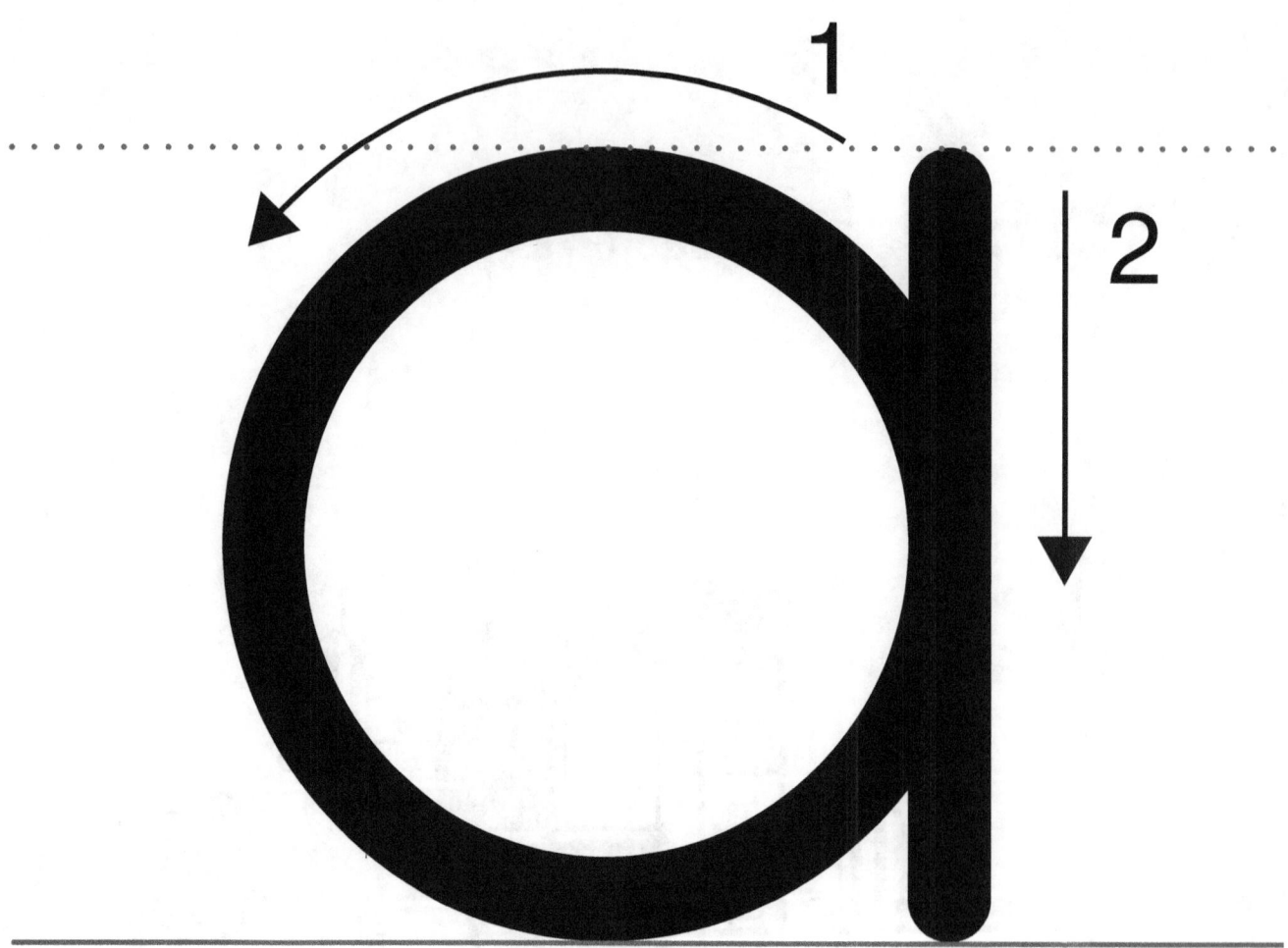

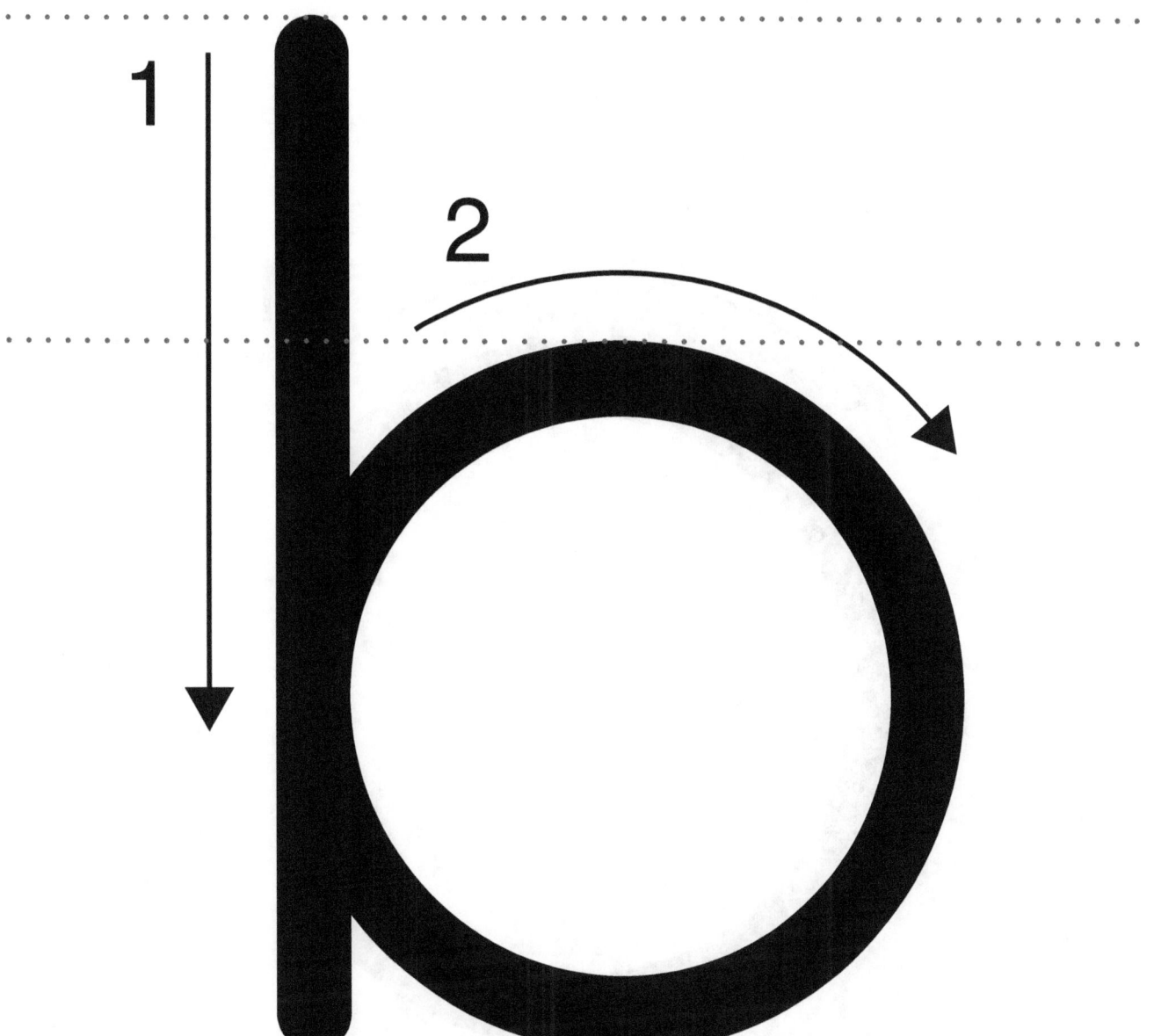

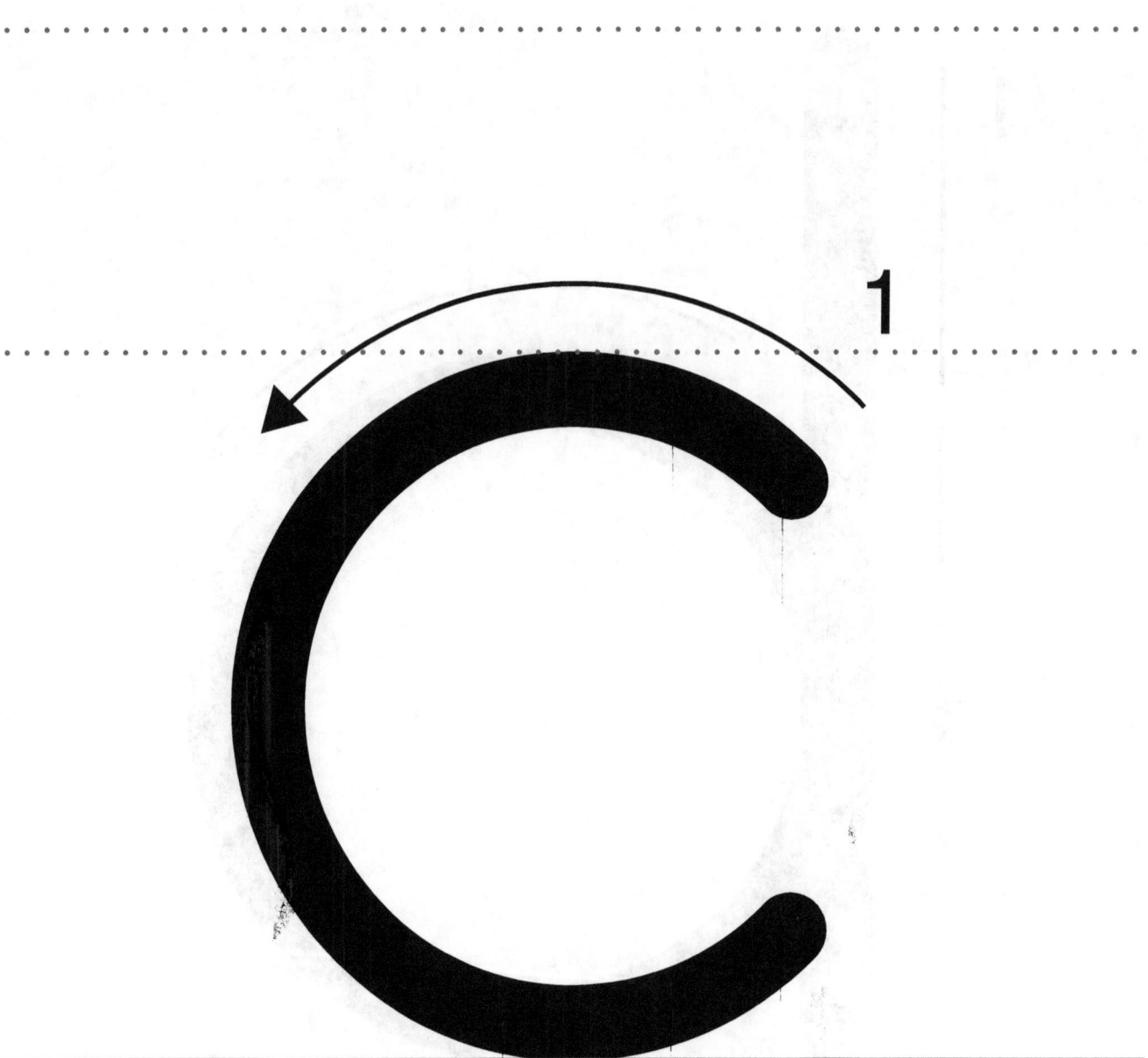

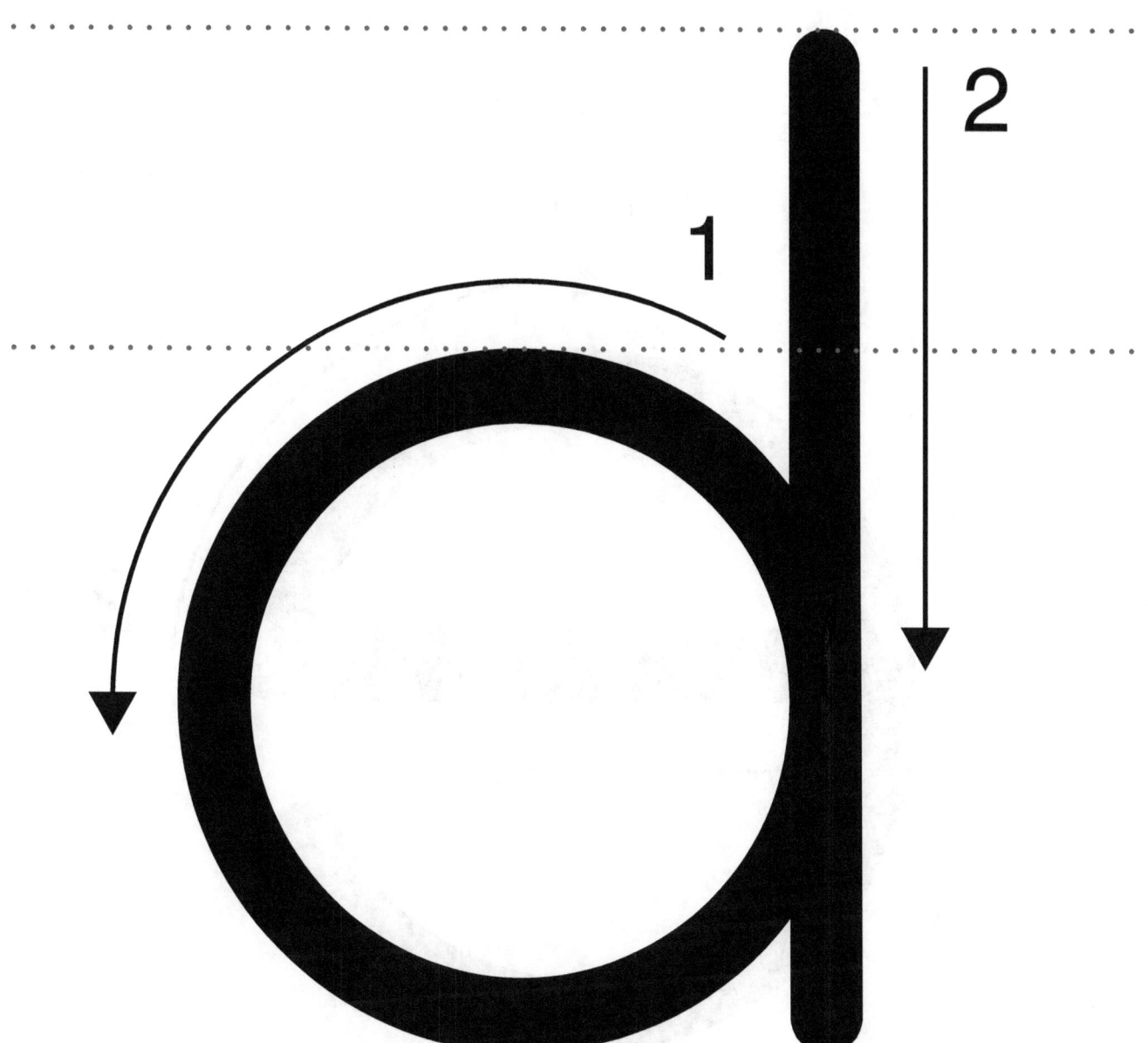

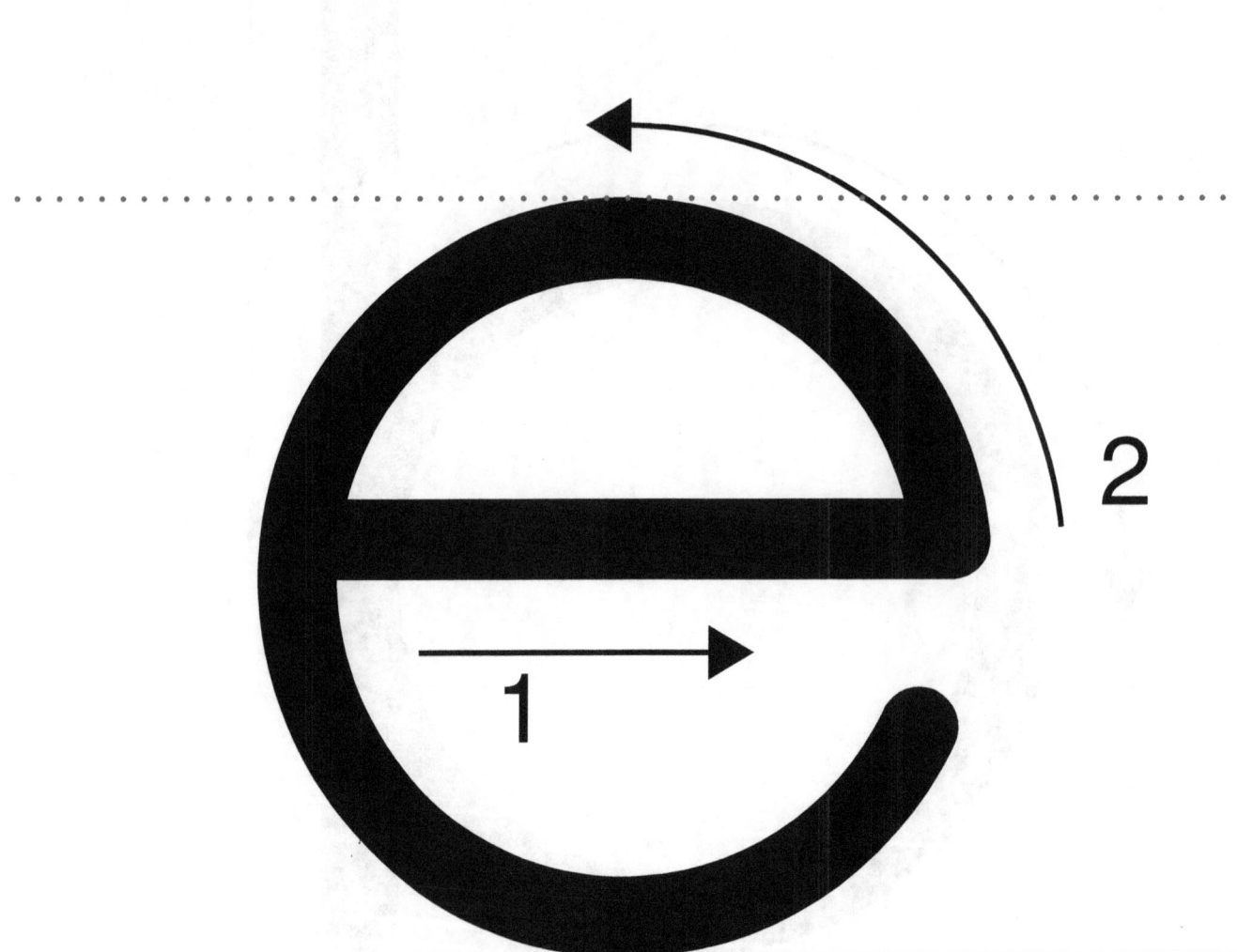

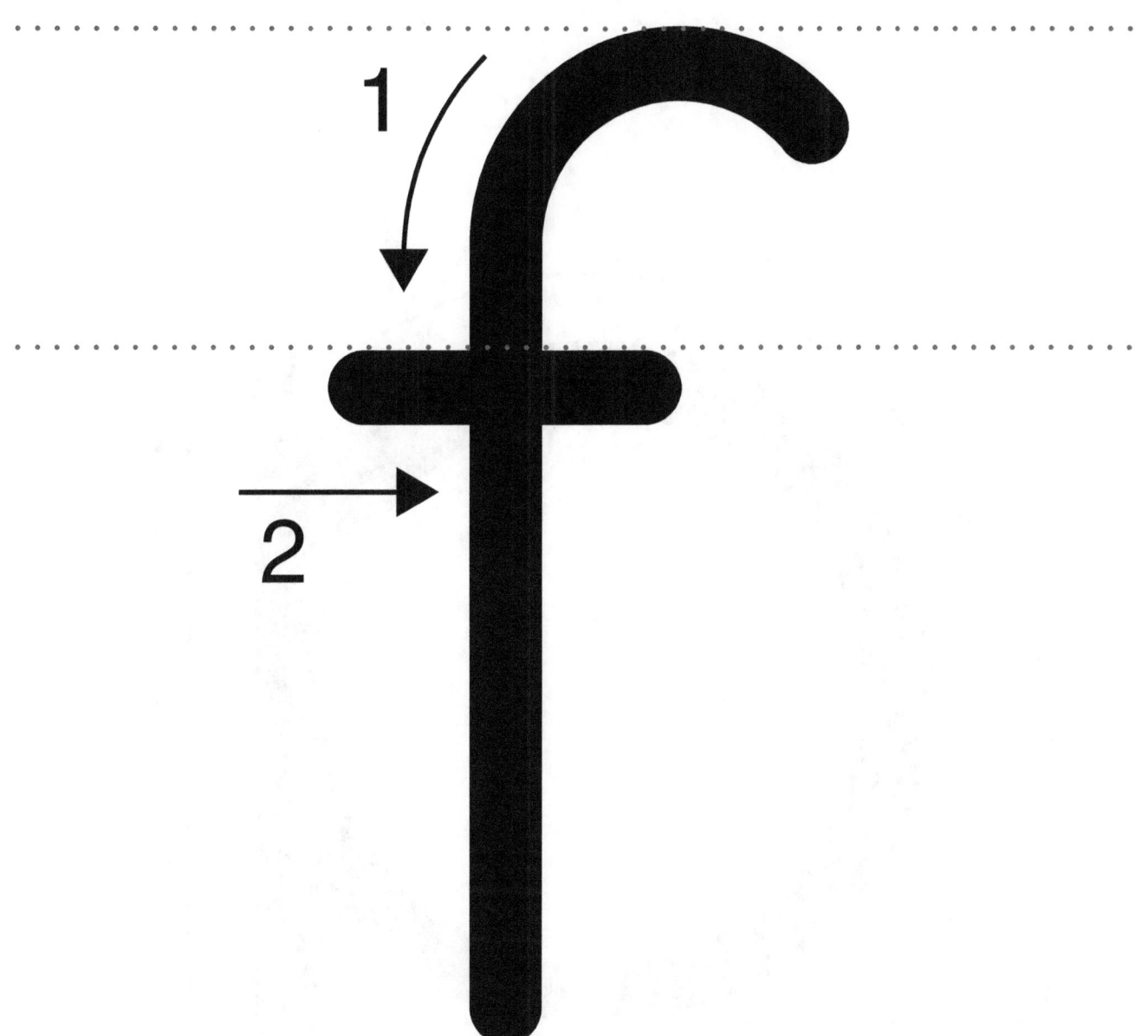

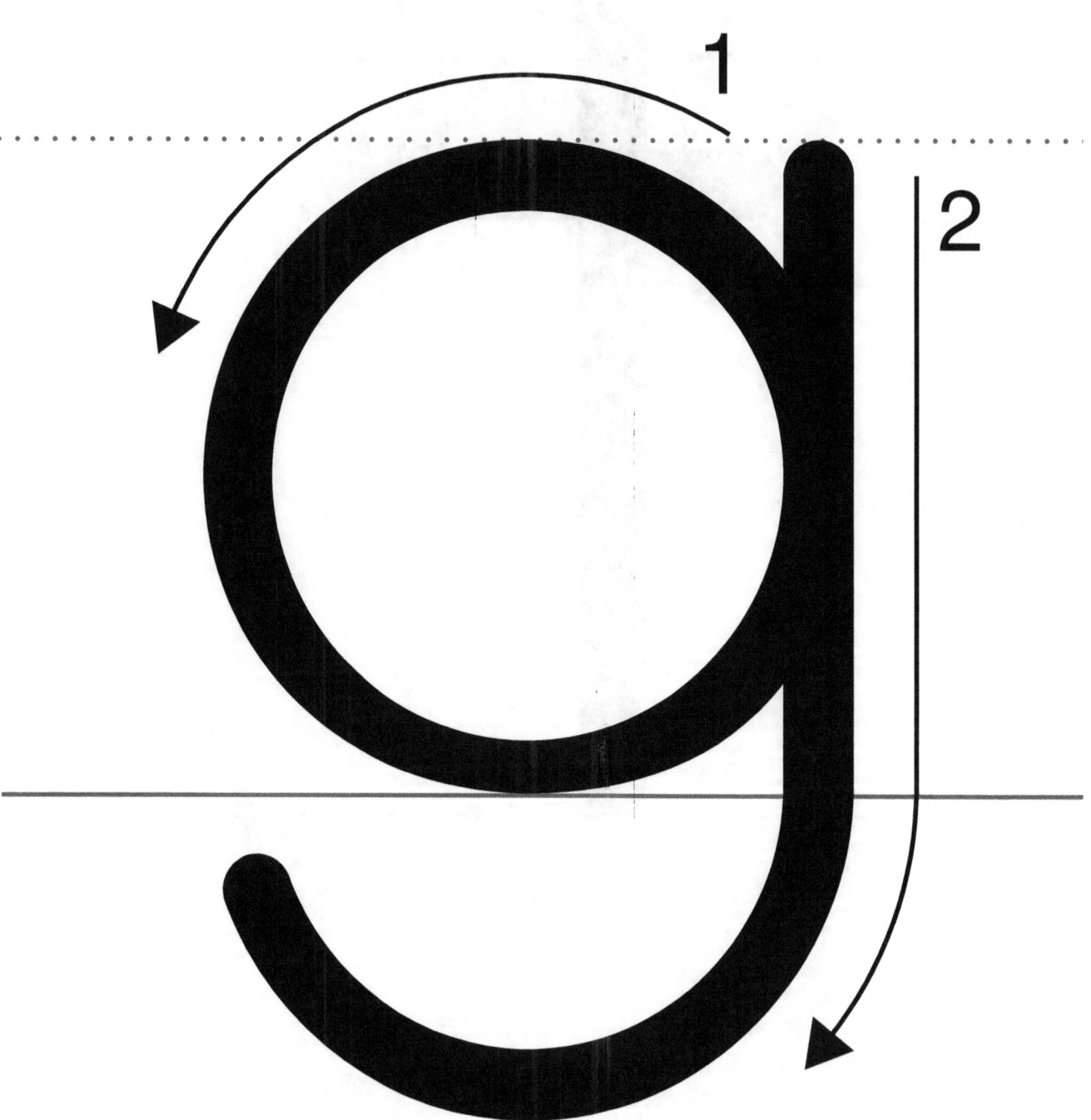

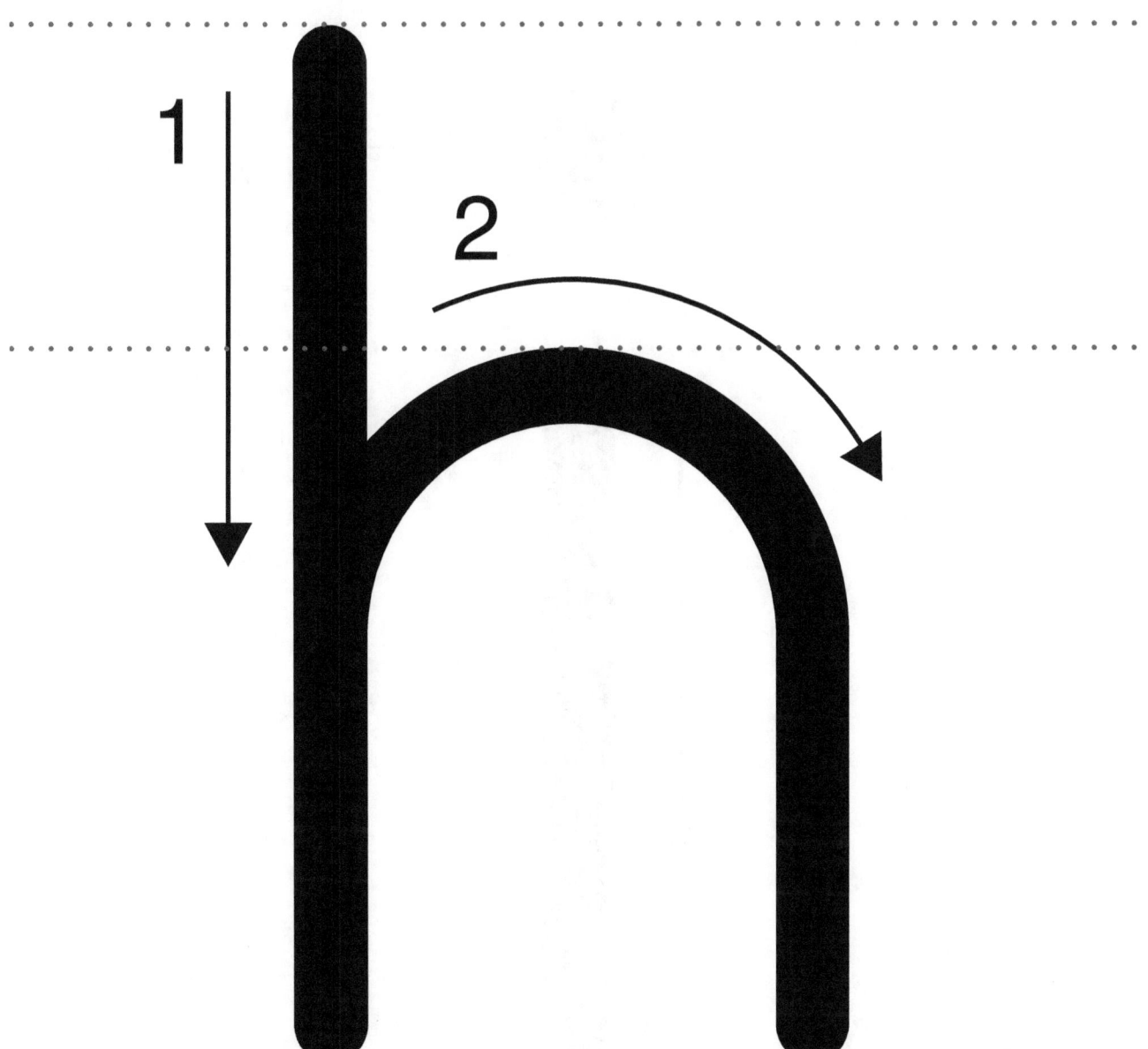

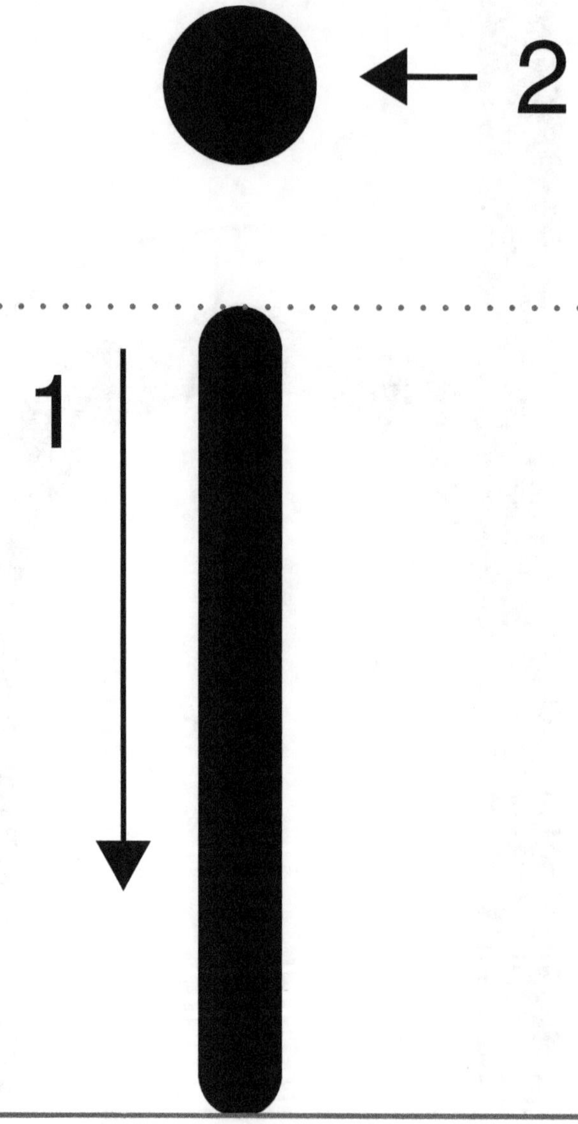

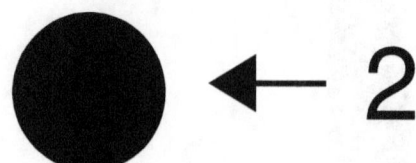

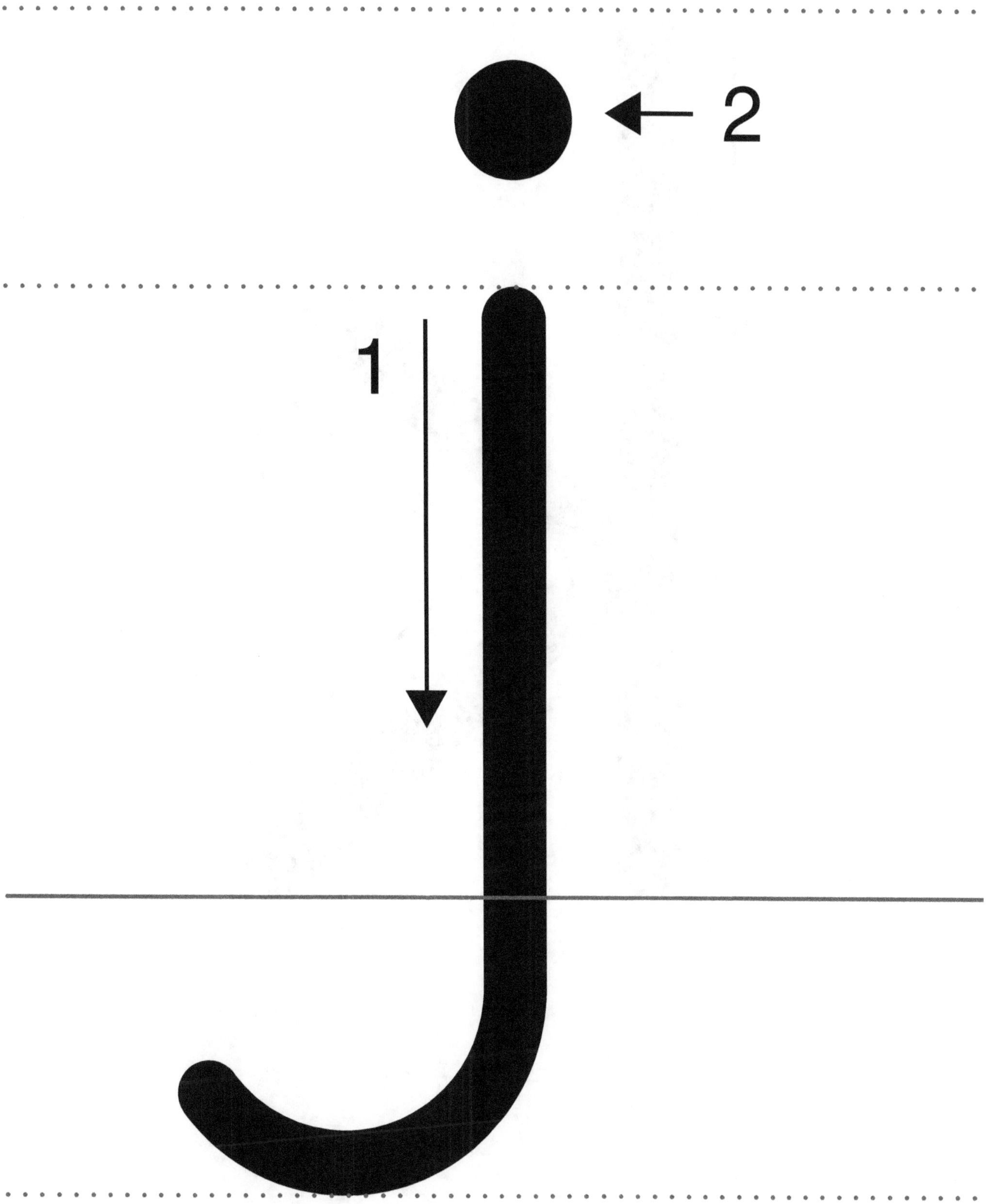

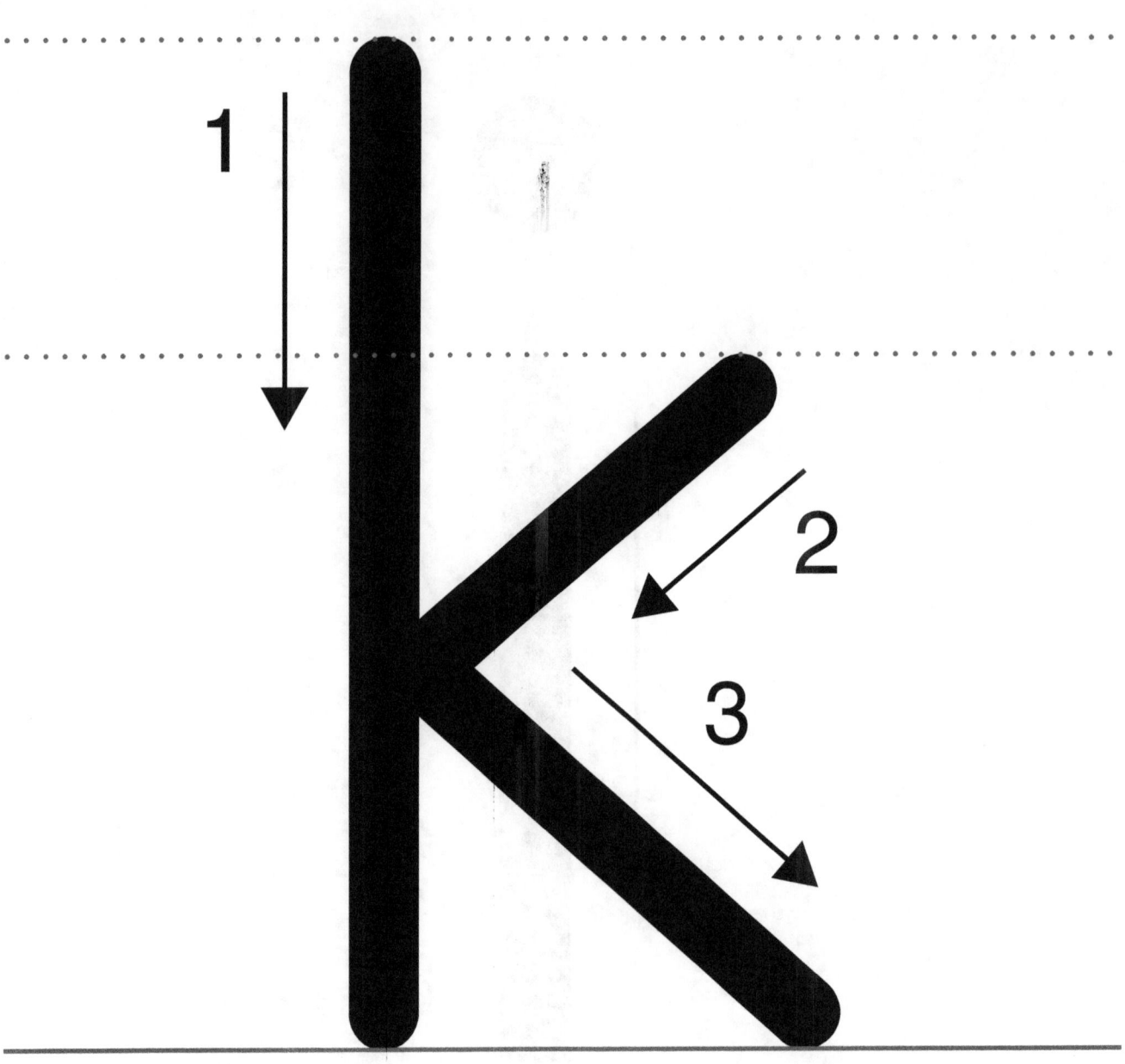

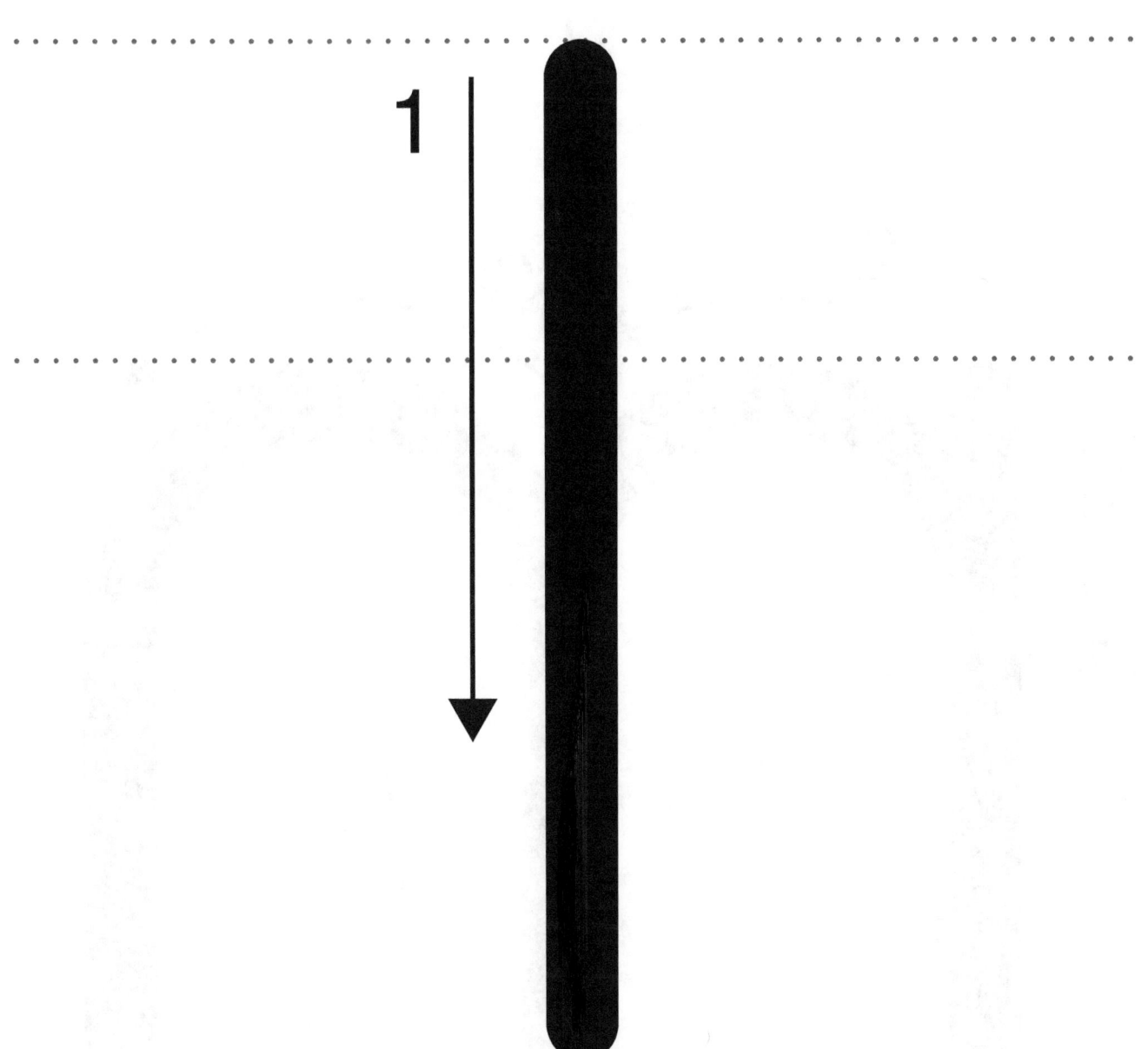

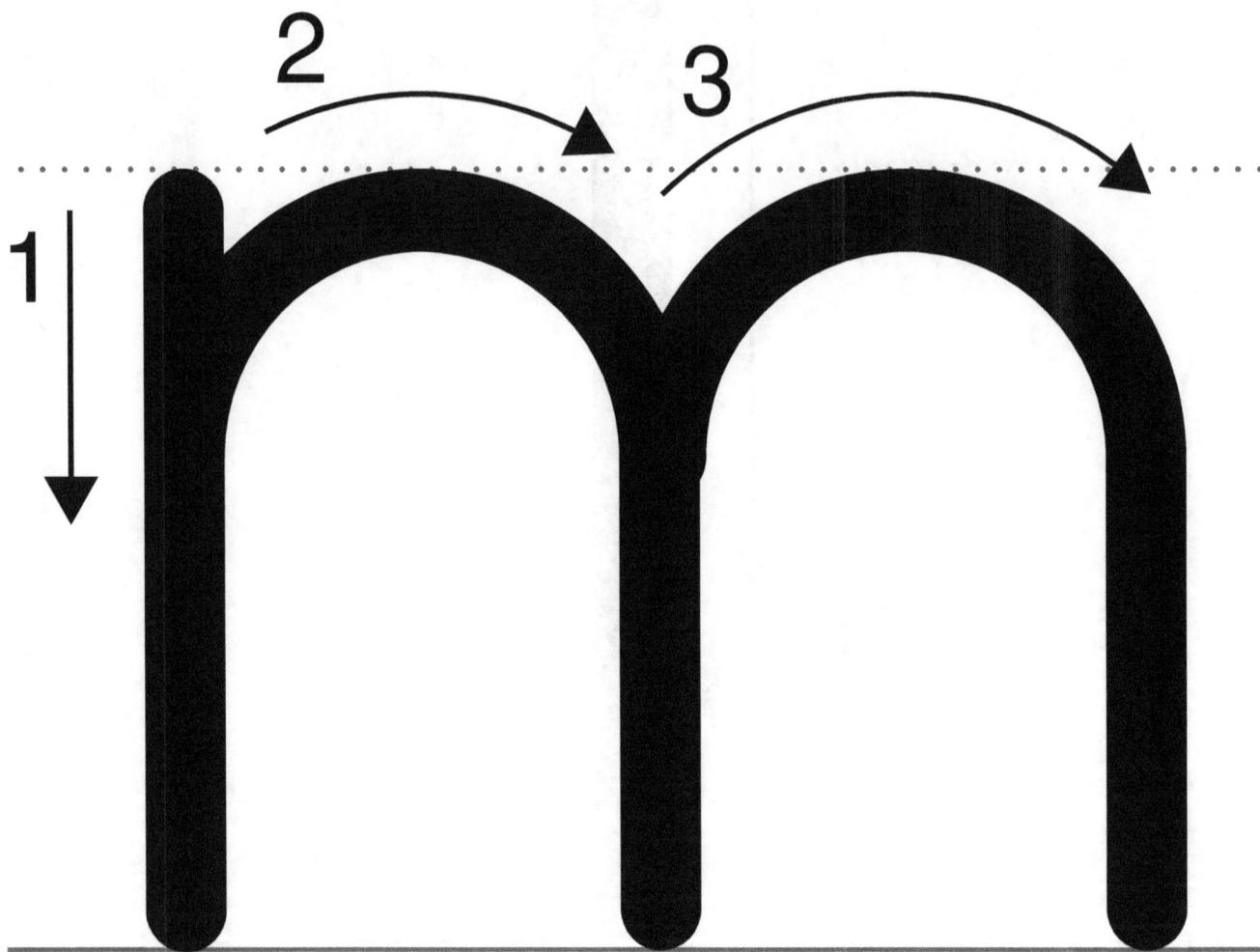

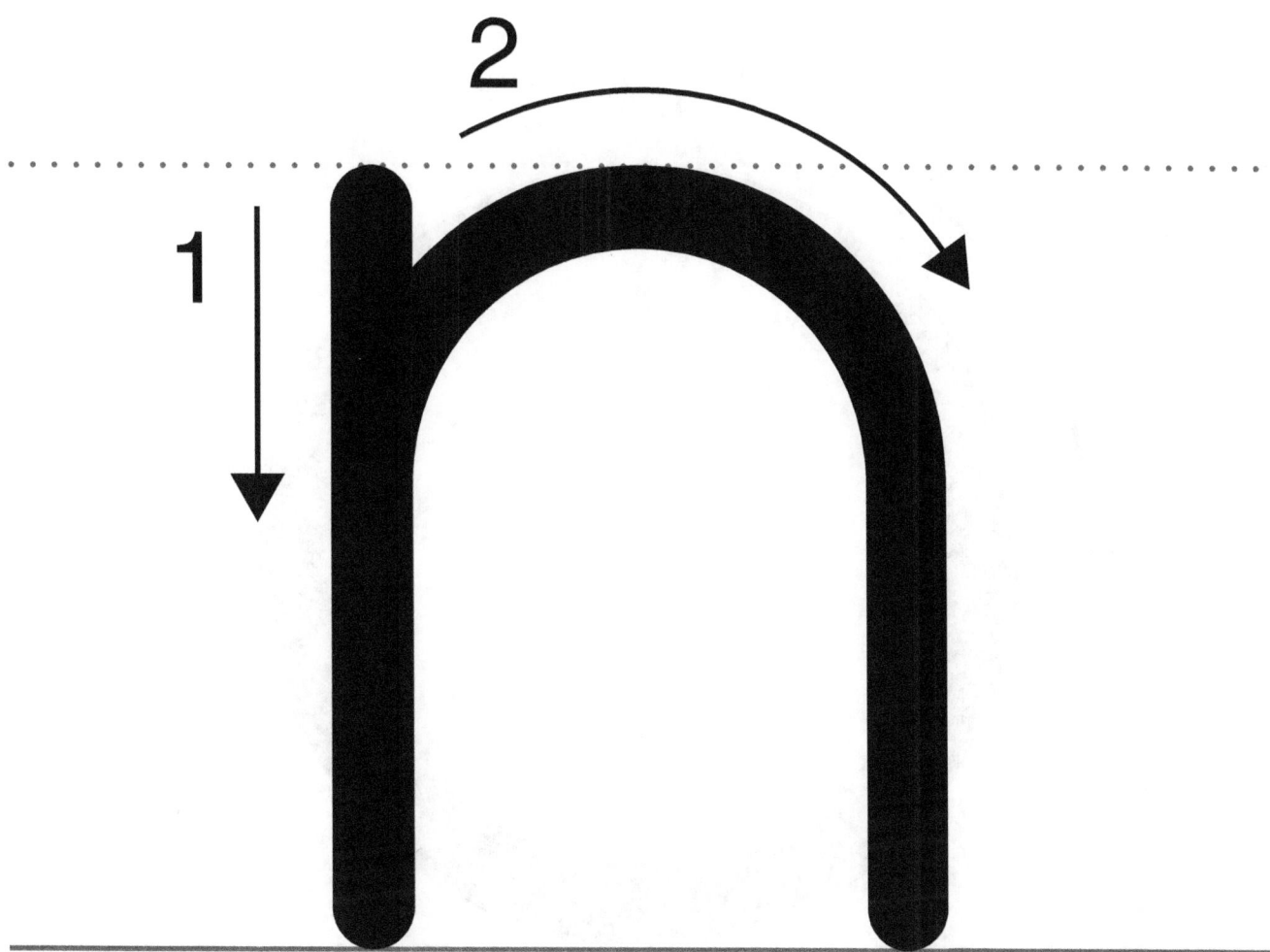

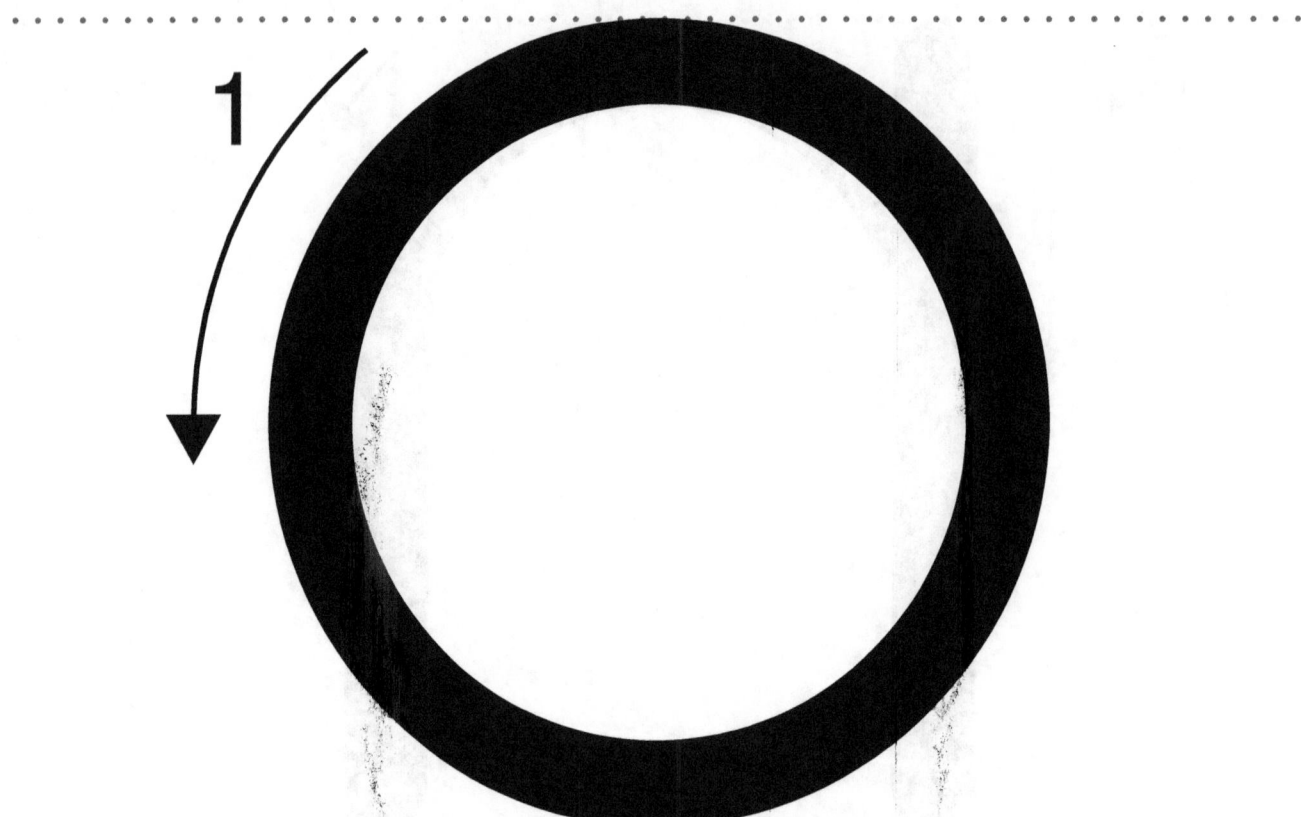

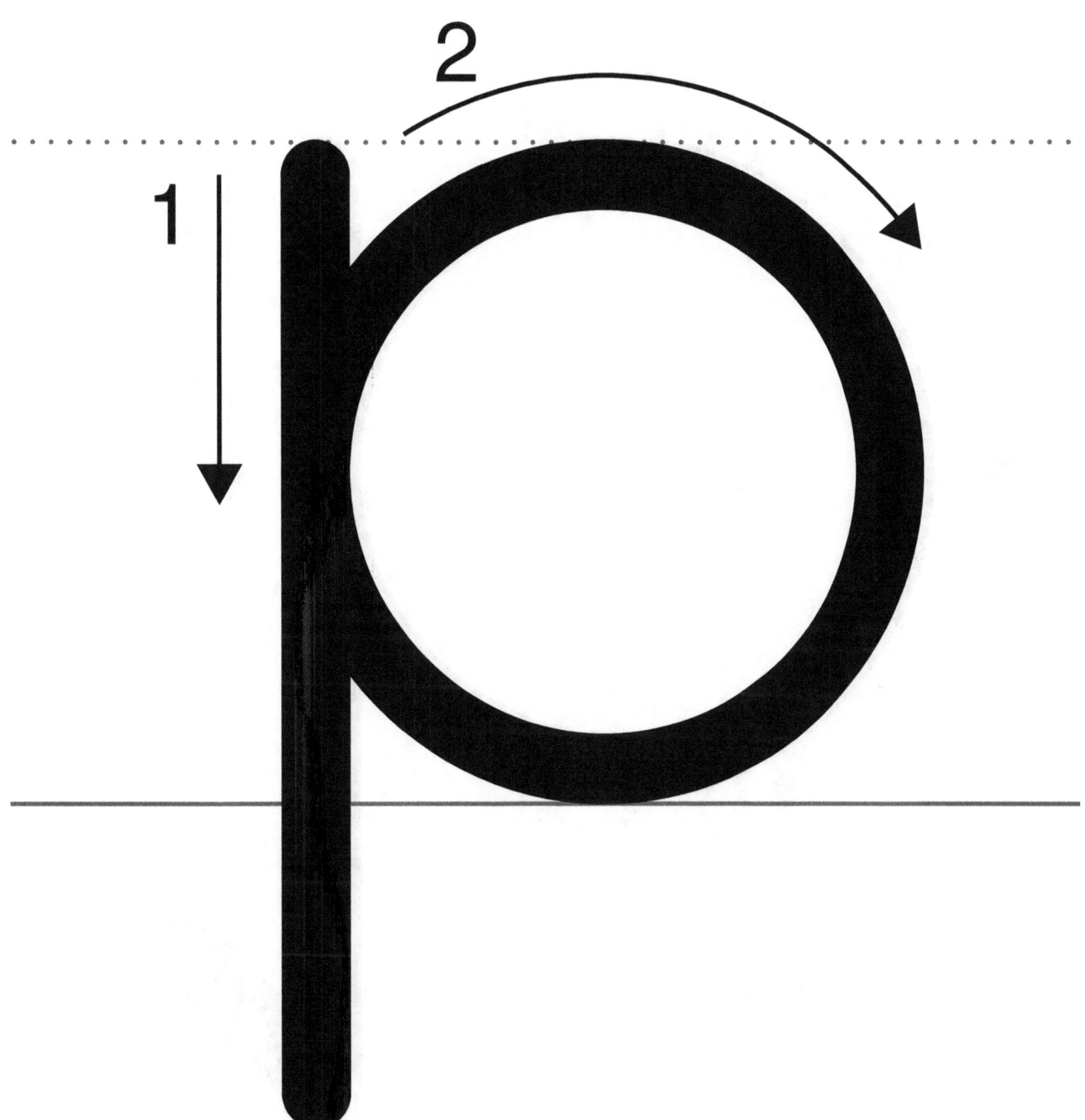

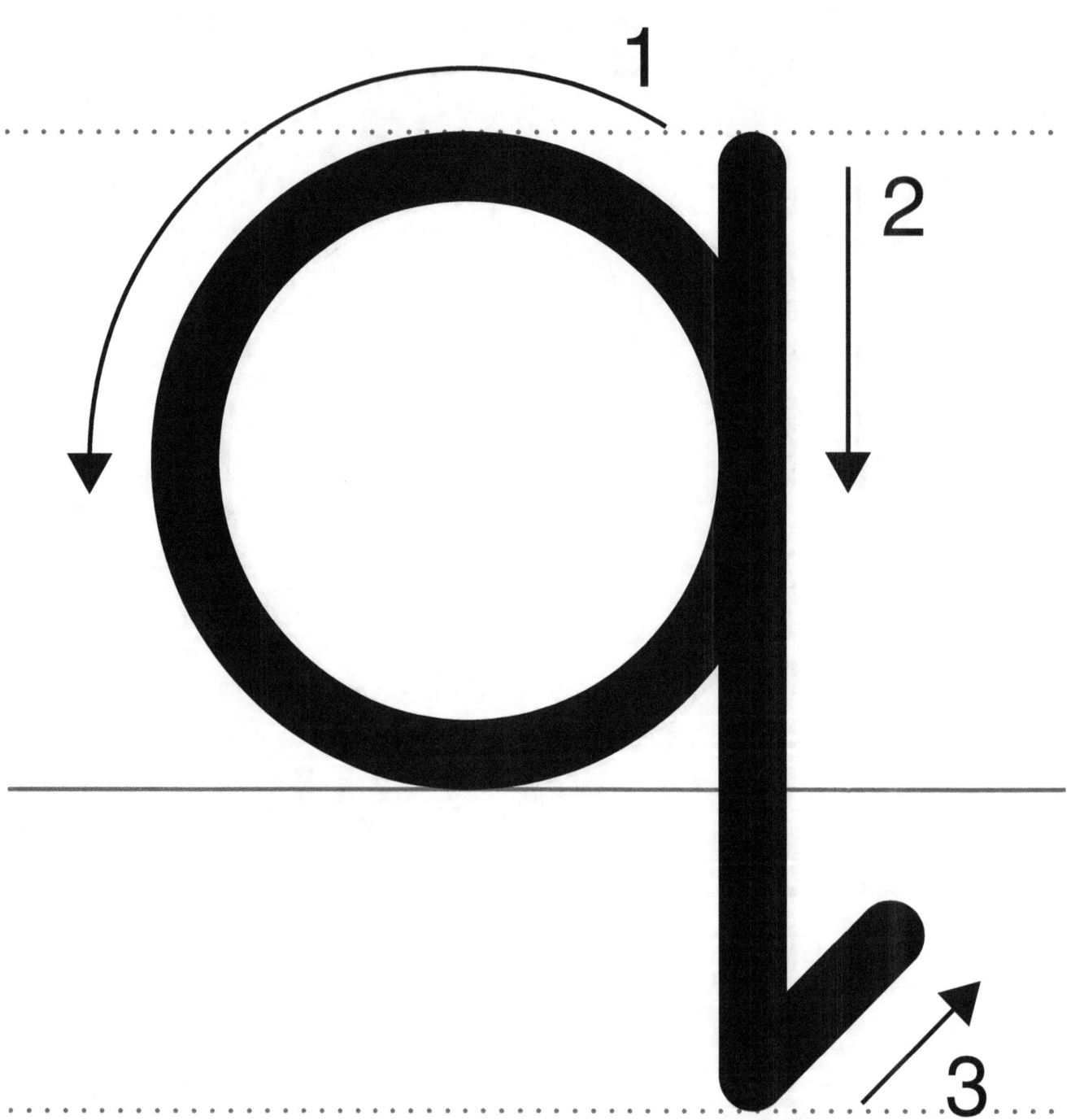

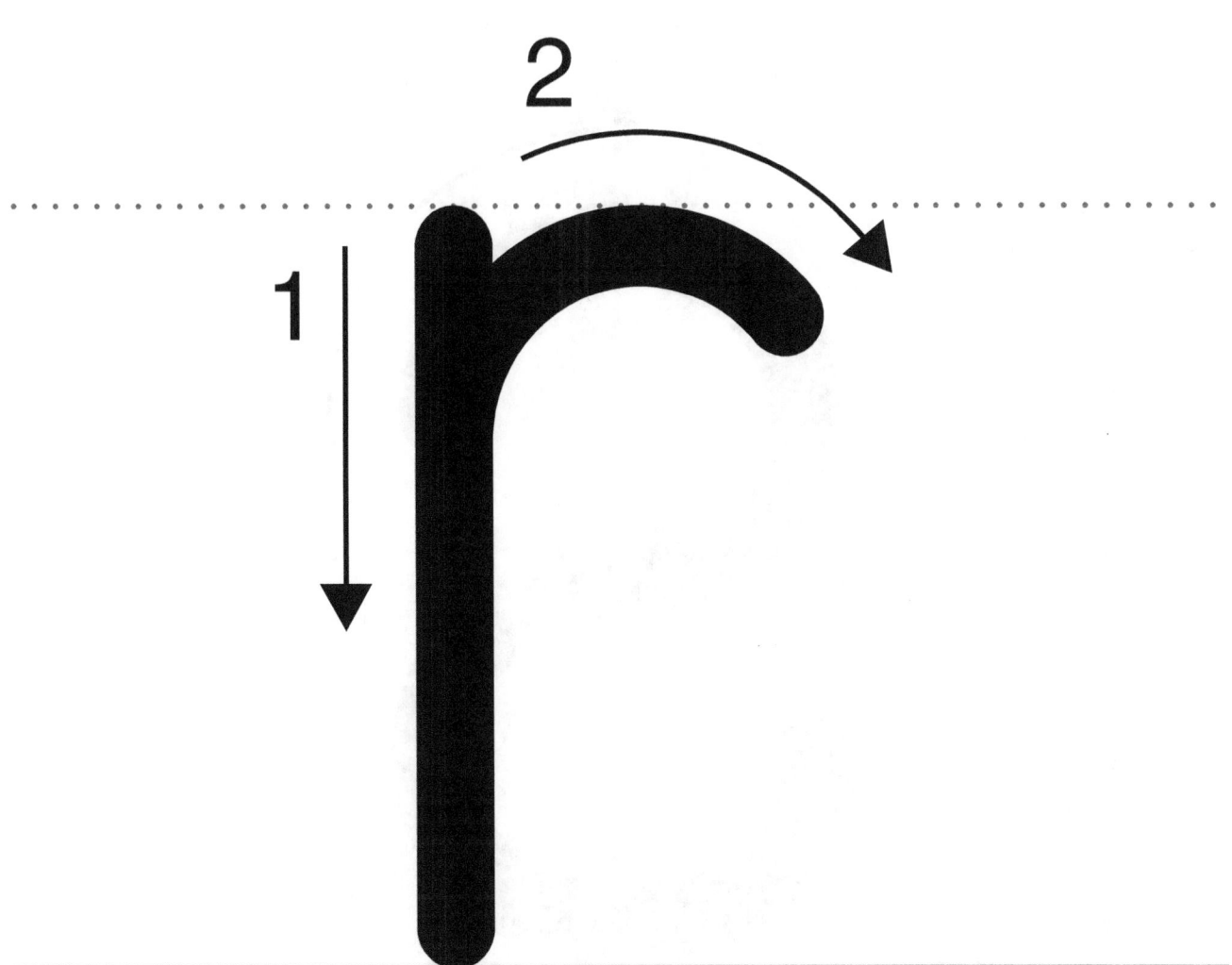

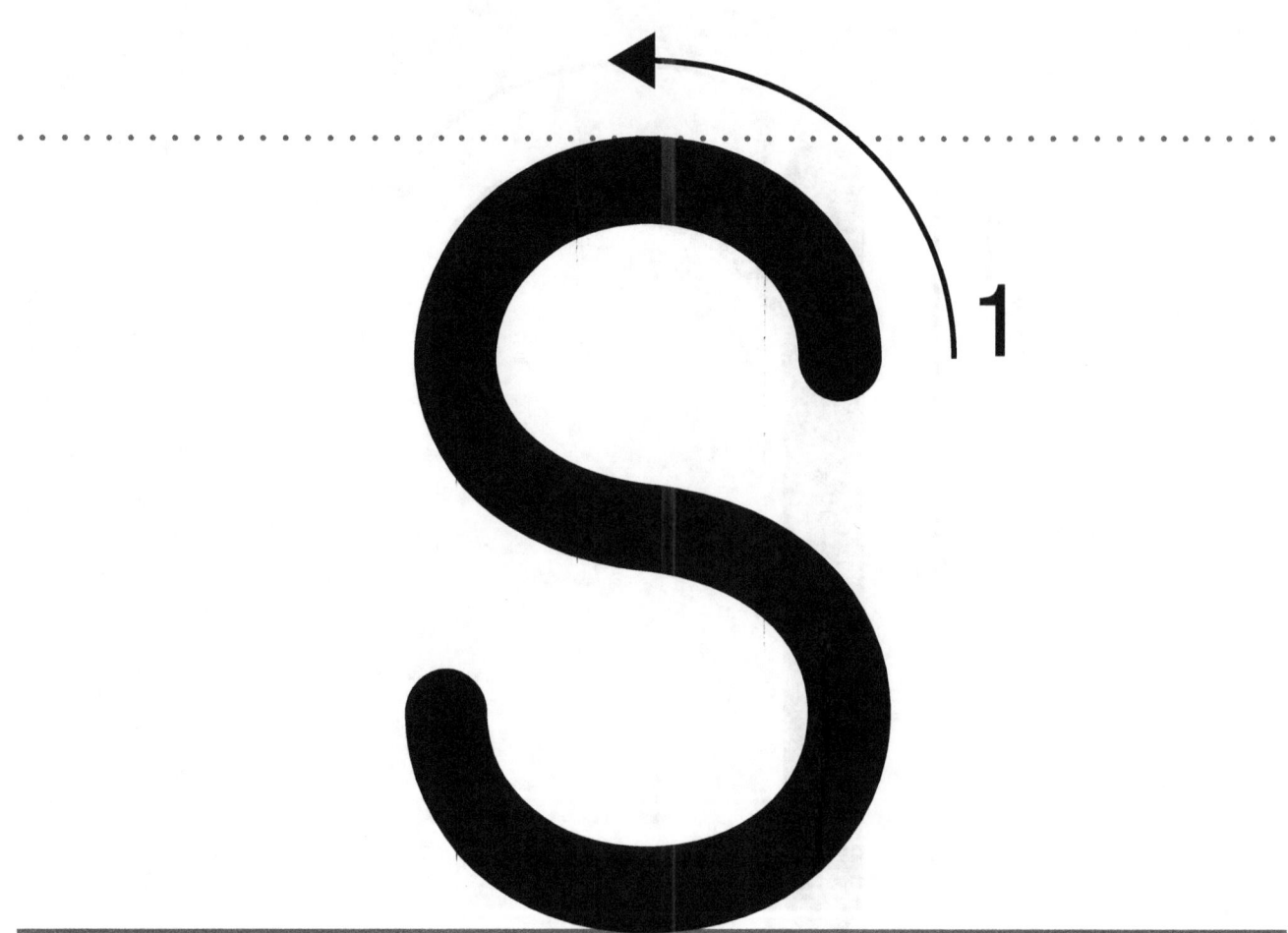

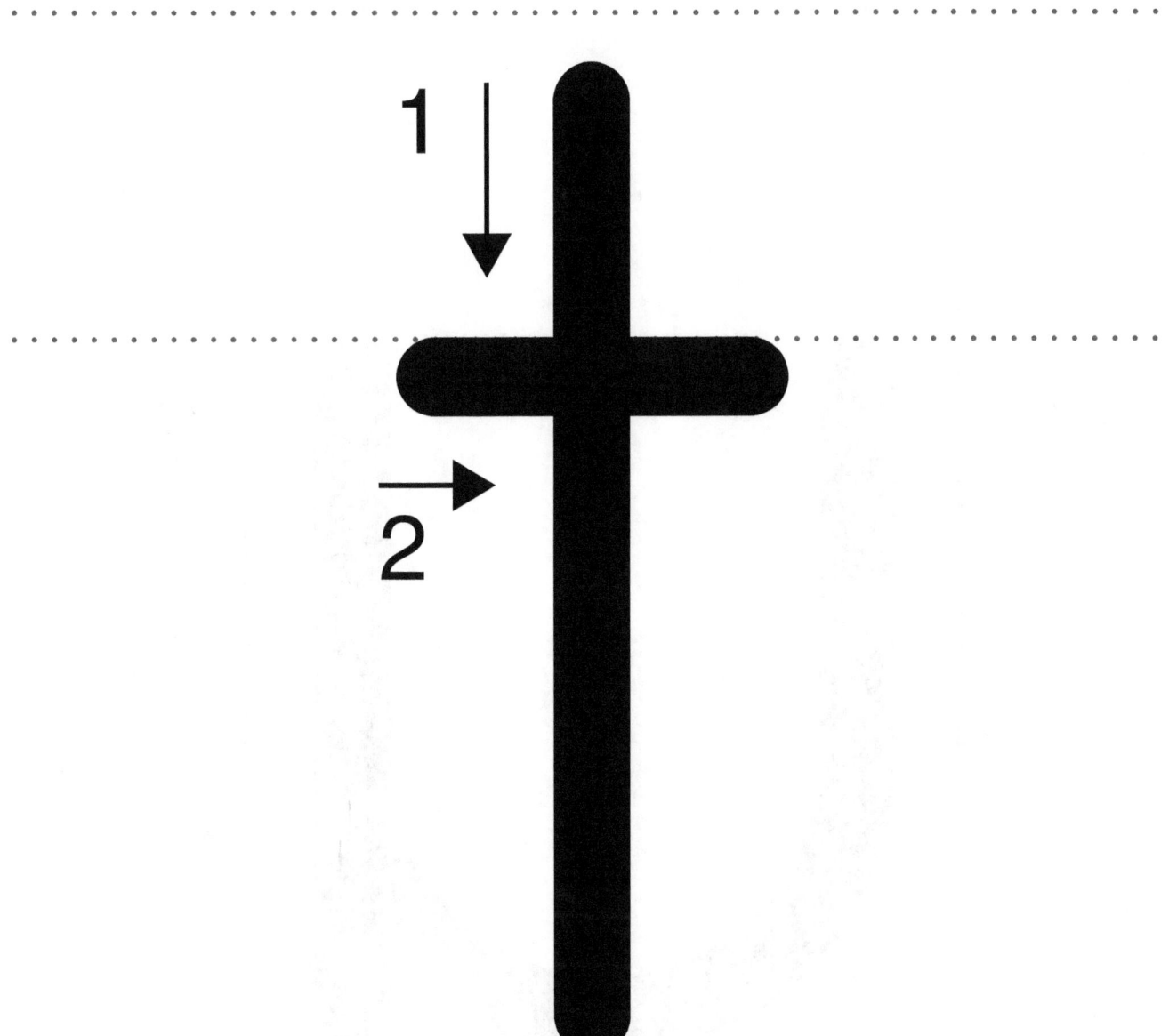

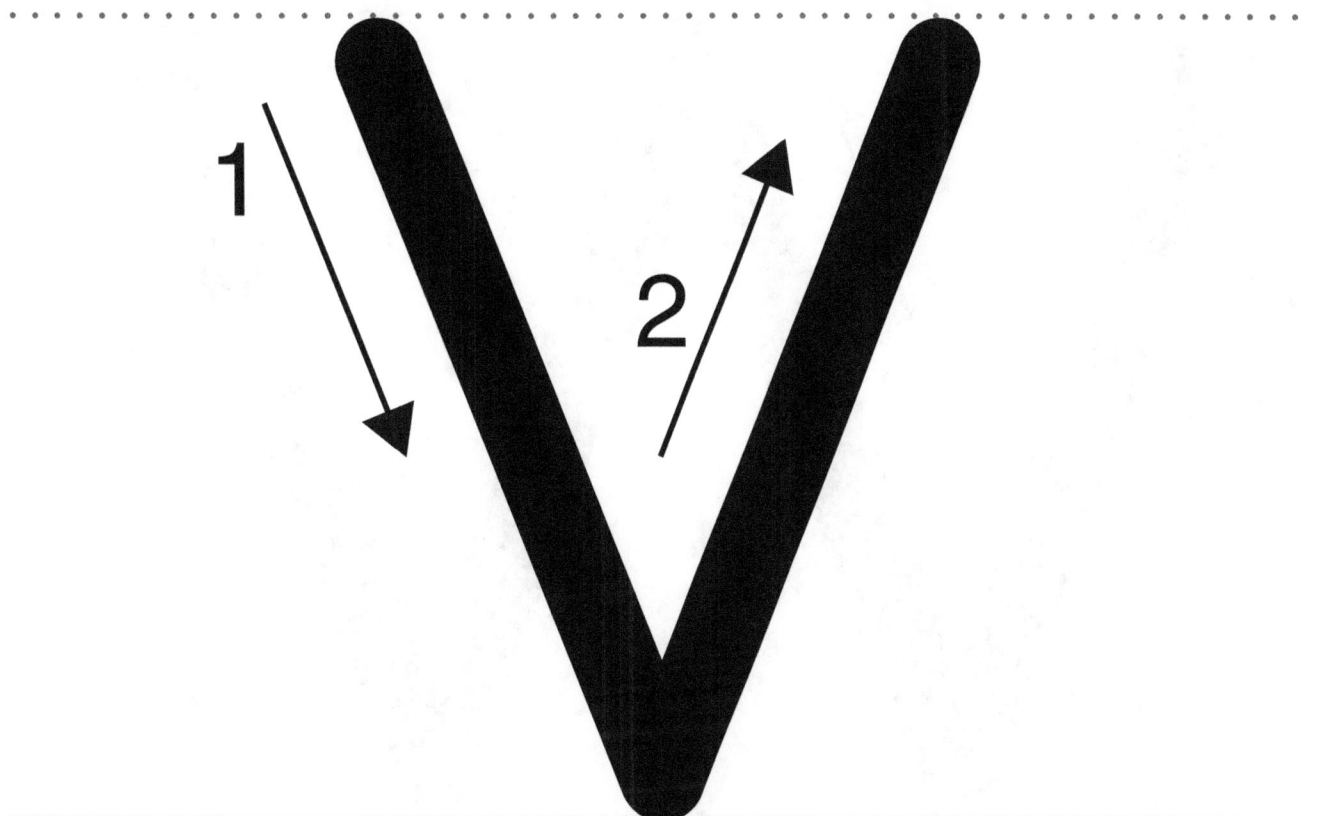

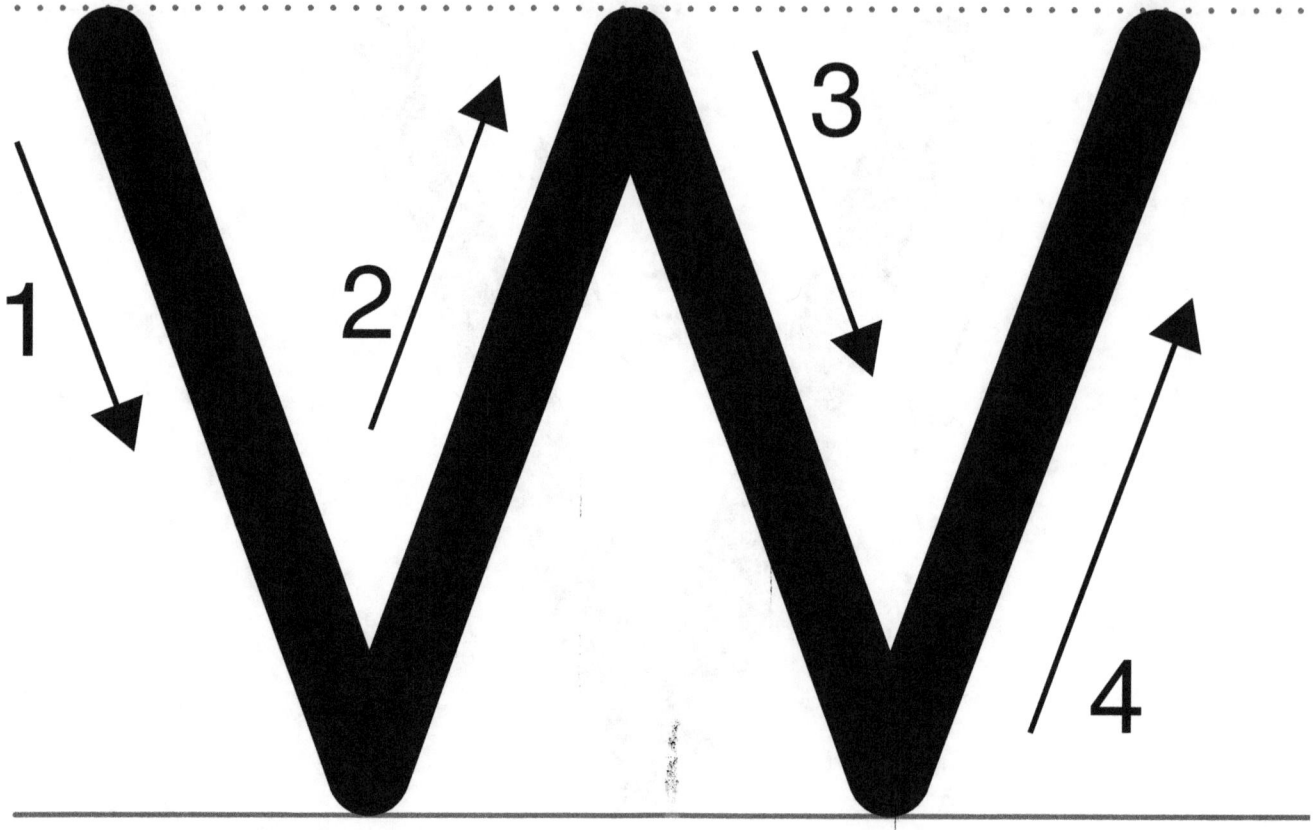

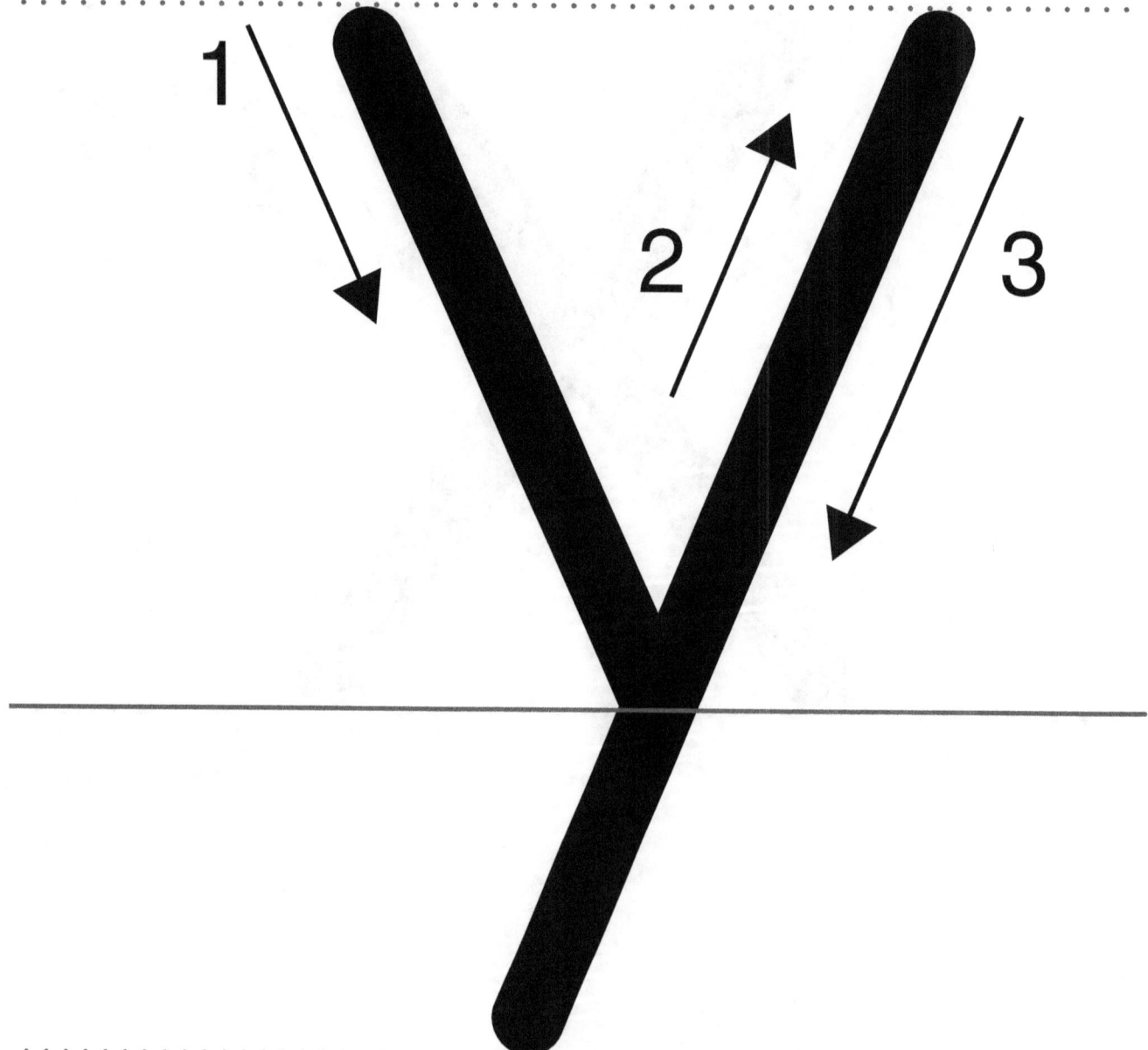

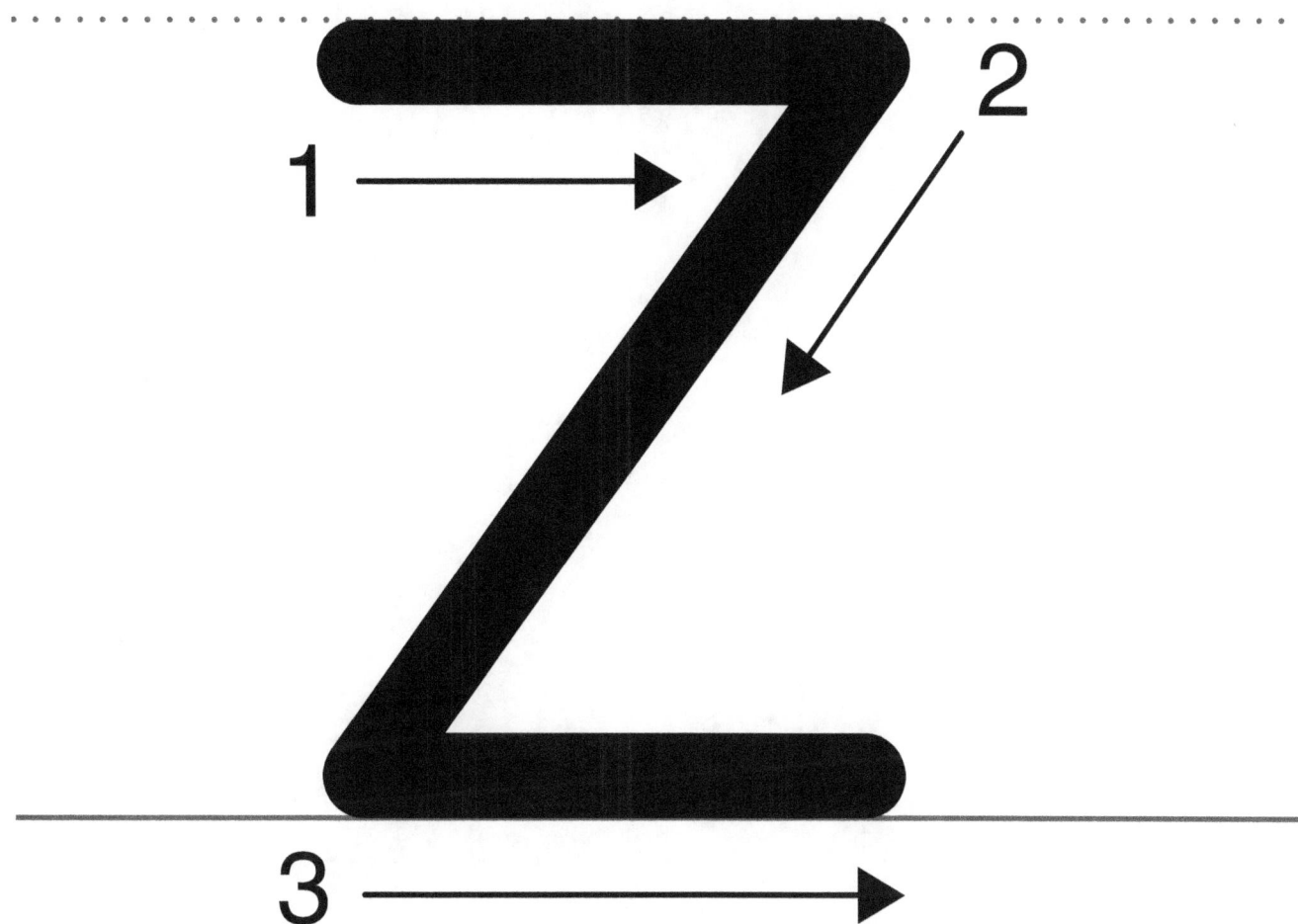

Letter Trace

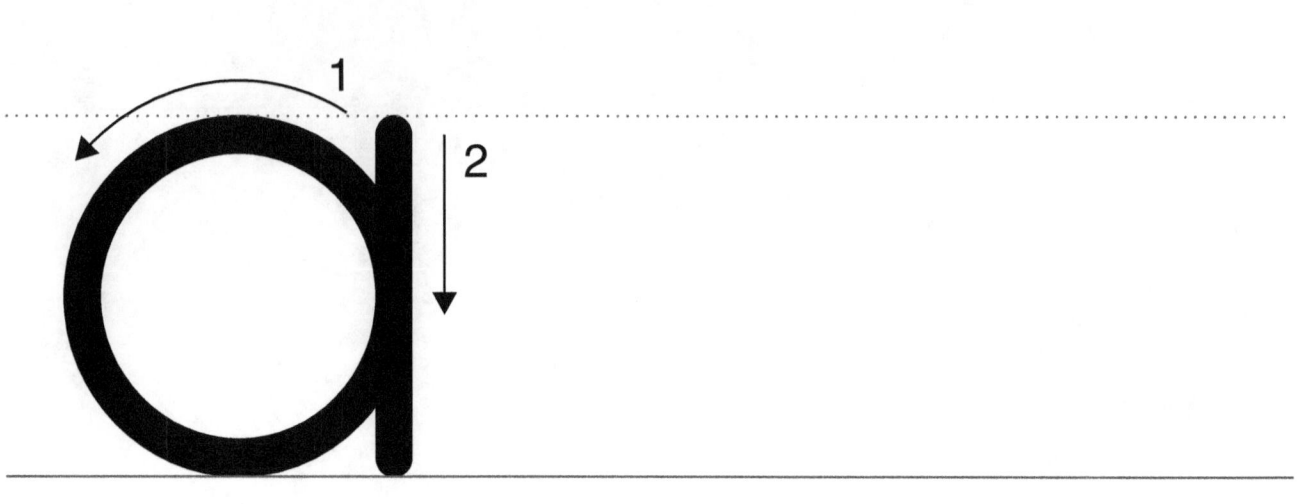

annie ape ate ants

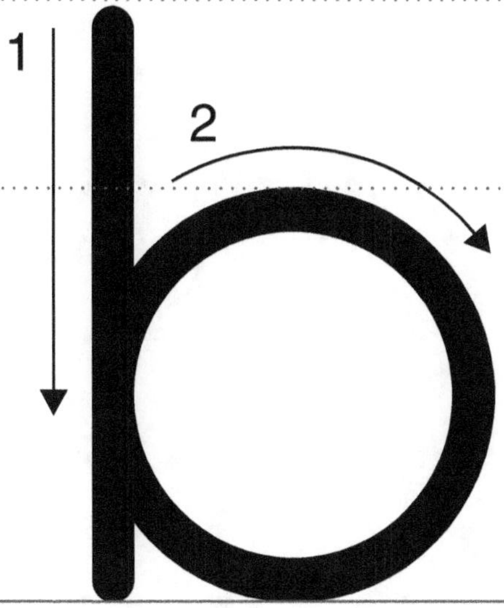

1 2

b b b b b b b b b b b b

b b b b b b b b b b b b

b b b b b

b b b b b

b b b b b

benny bear bakes buns

c c c c c c c c c c c c c

c c c c c c c c c c

c c c c

c c c c

connie cougar

combs cubs

dewdney dragon

digs dungeons

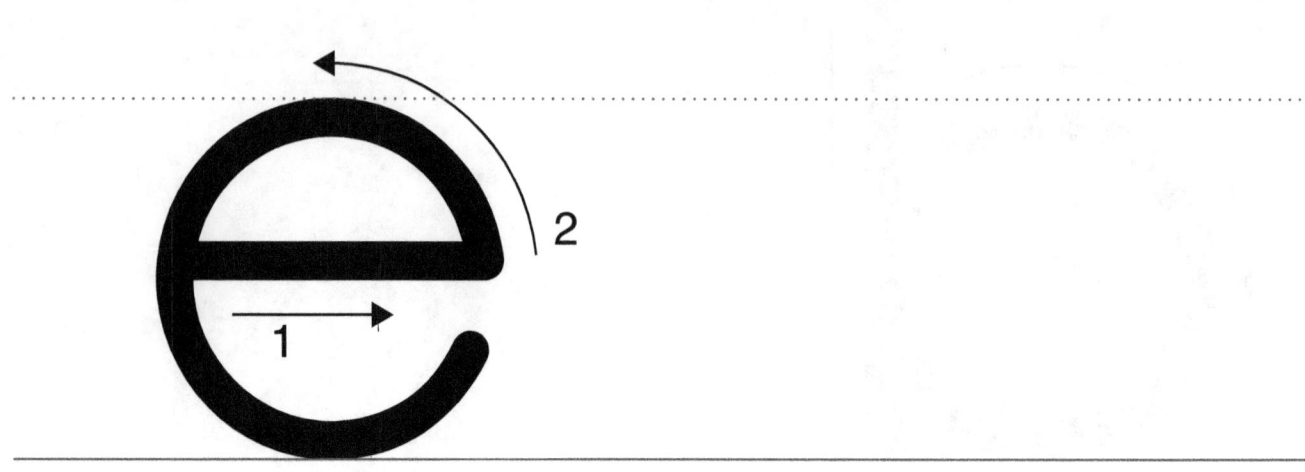

eeeeeeeeeeee

eeeeeeeeeeee

e e e e

e e e e

eadie elk

eats eggplants

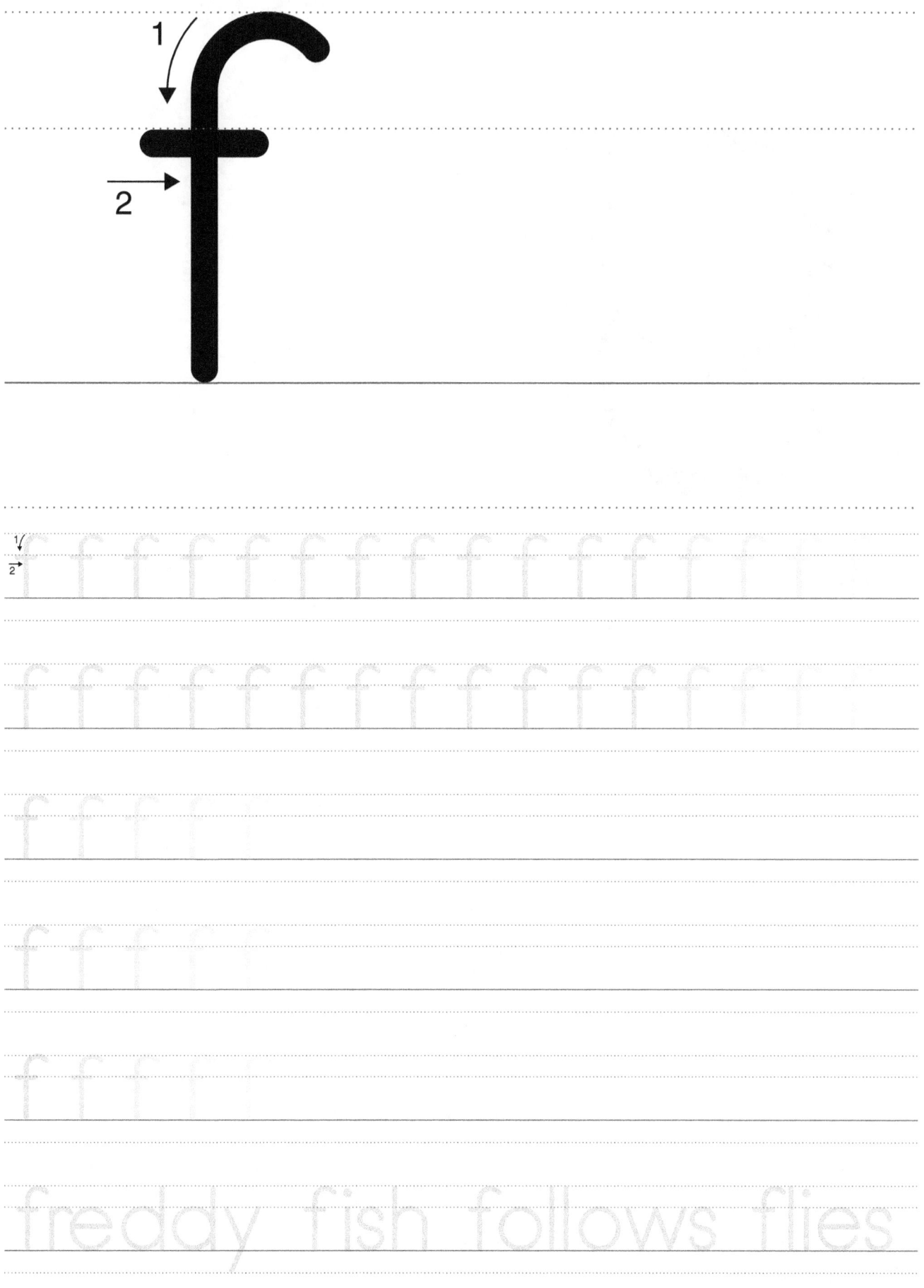

freddy fish follows flies

gertie goose gathers

gardenias

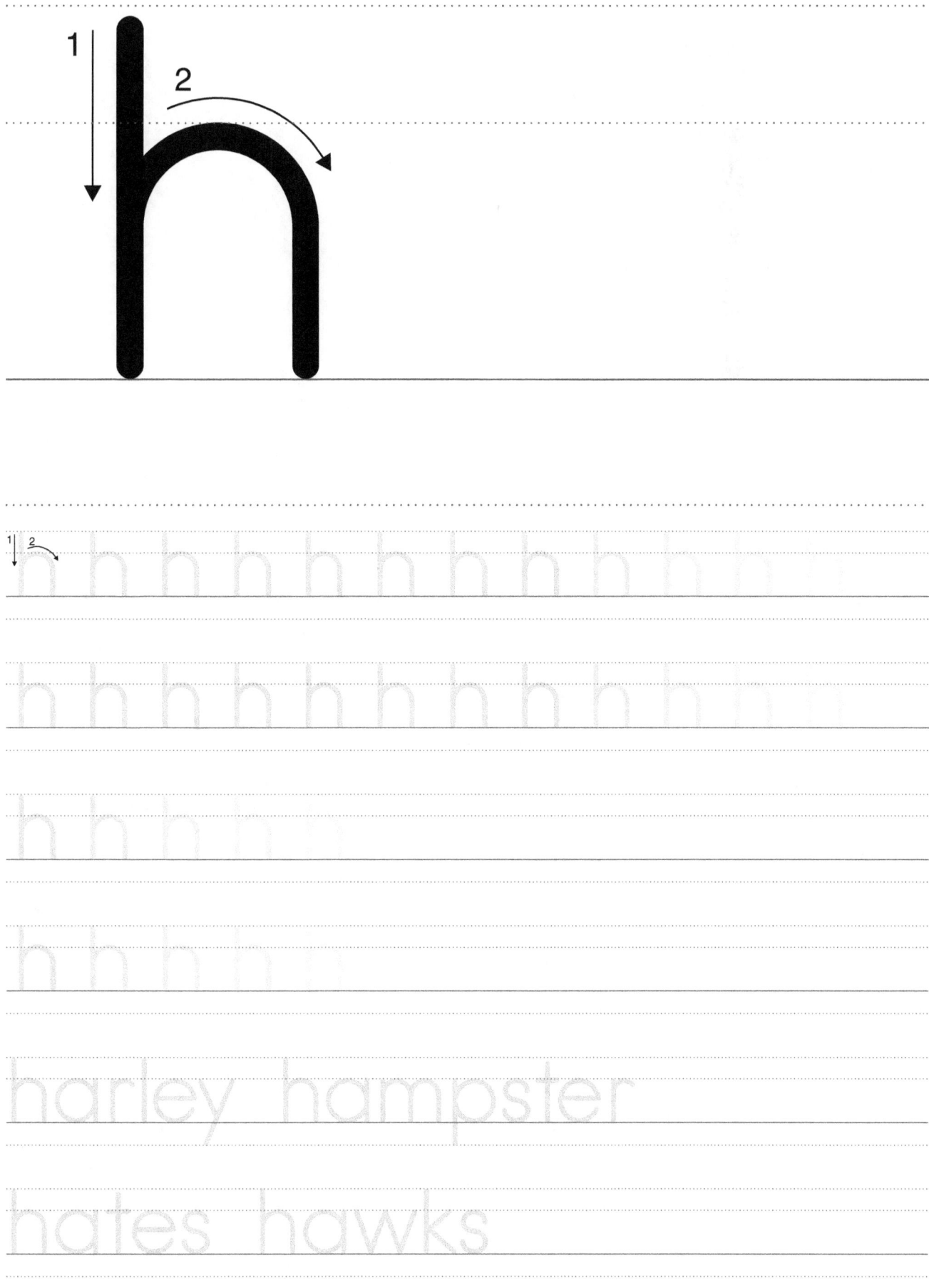

harley hampster

hates hawks

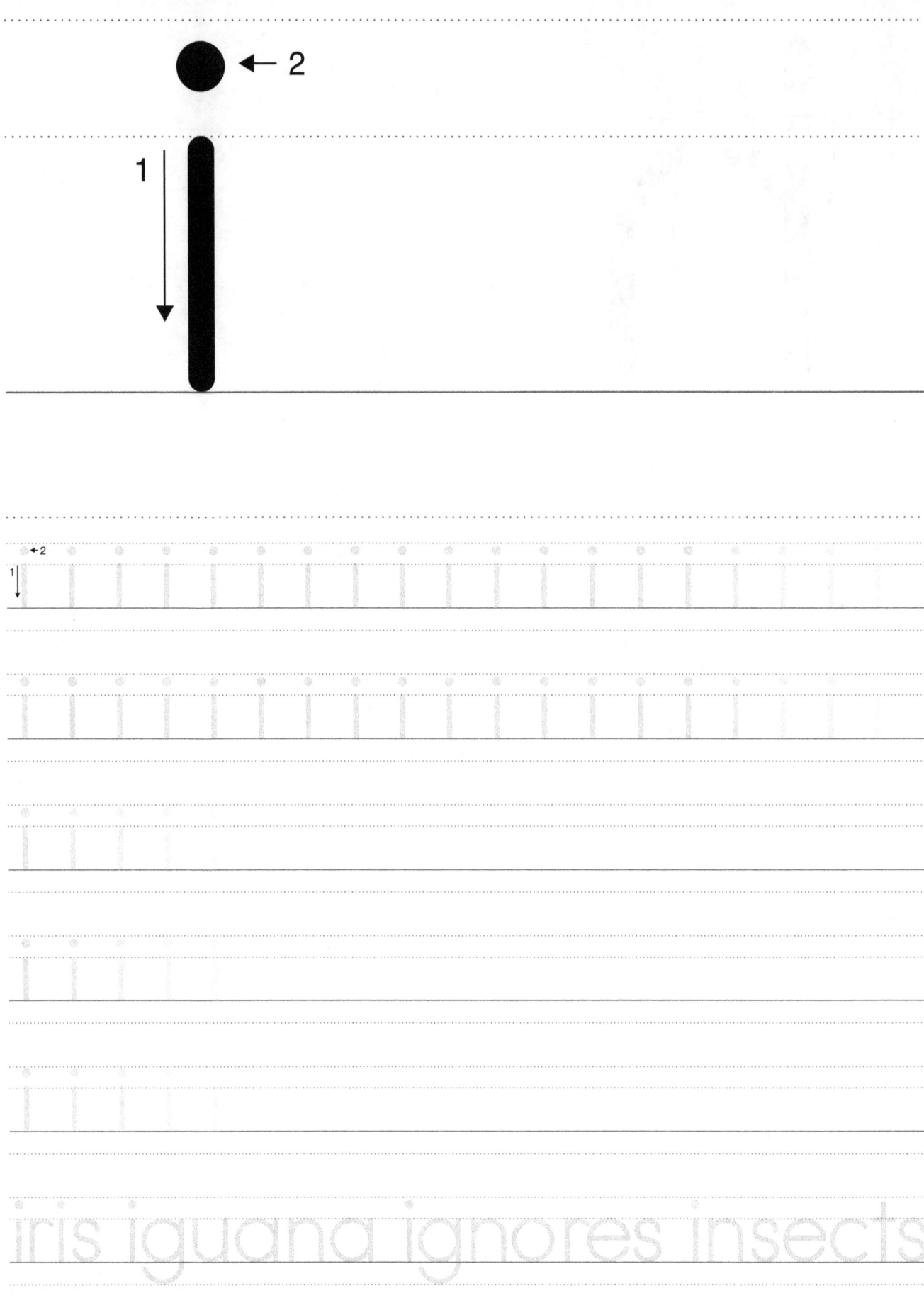

iris iguana ignores insects

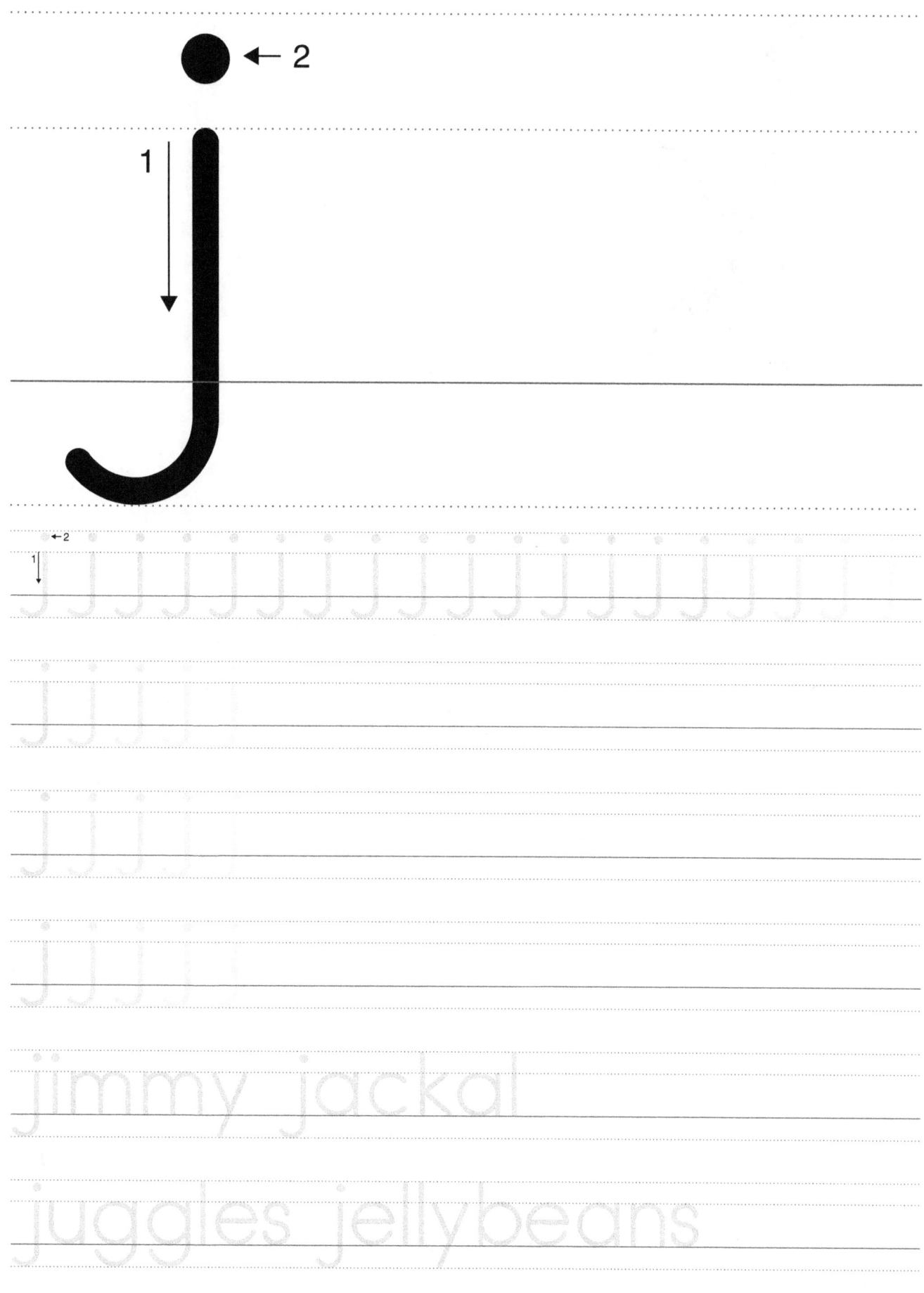

jjjjjjjjjjjjjj

jjj

jjj

jjj

jimmy jackal

juggles jellybeans

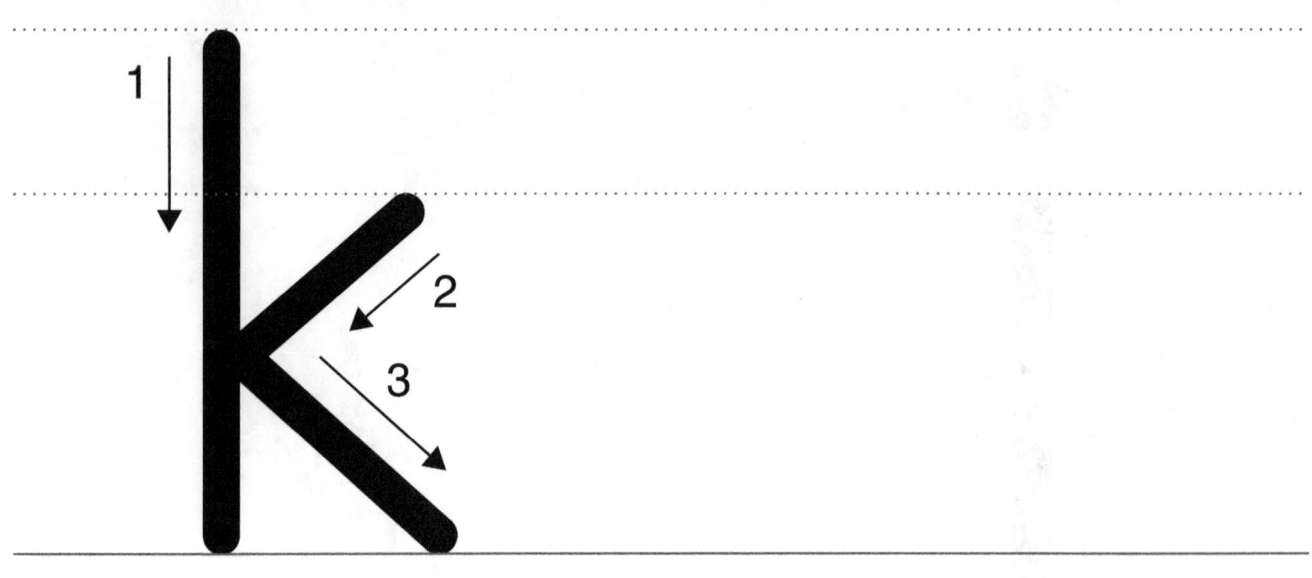

k k k k k k k k k k k k k k k k

k k k k k k k k k k k k k k k k

k k k k

k k k k

k k k k

kelly koala kicks kiwis

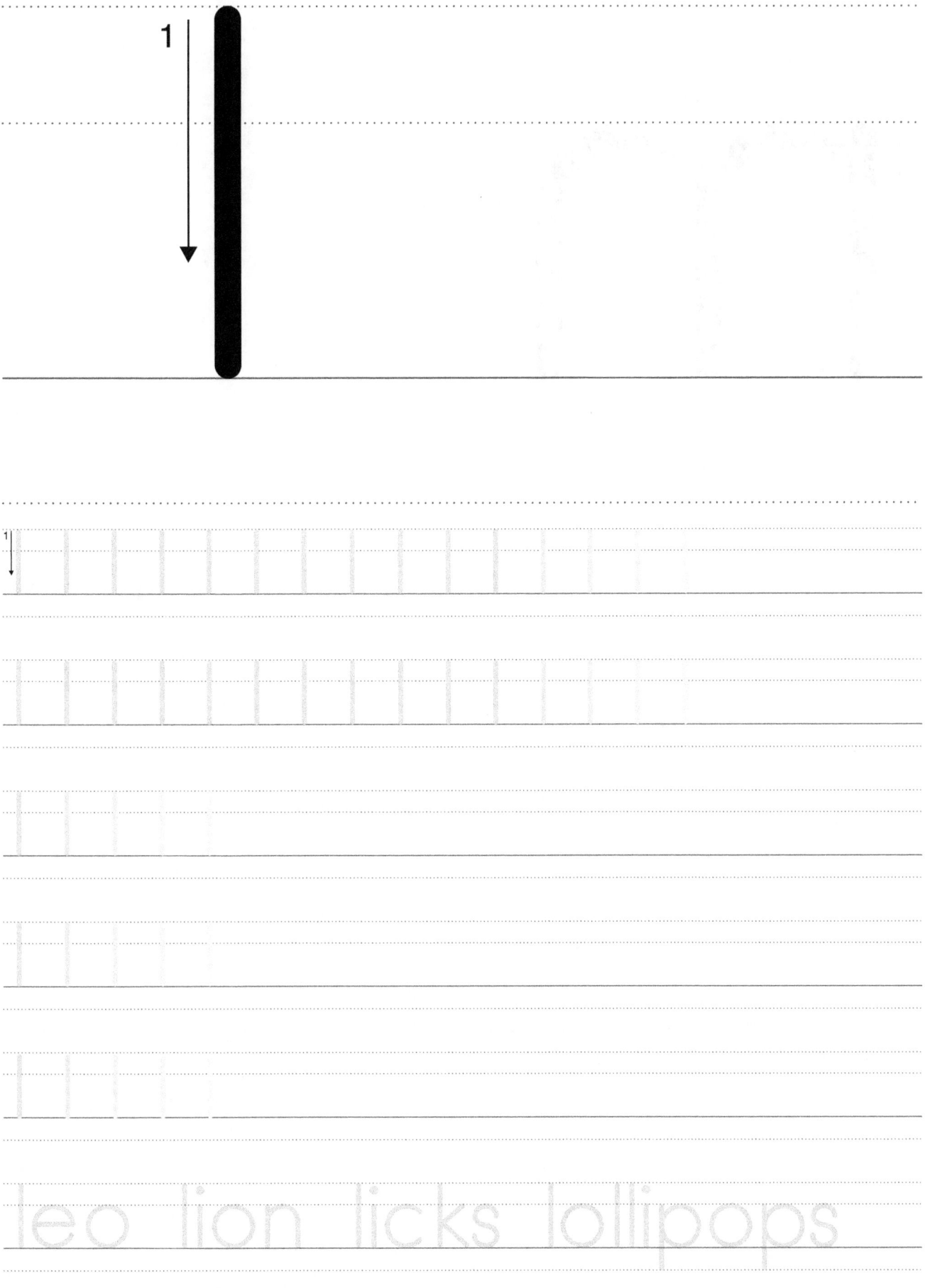

leo lion licks lollipops

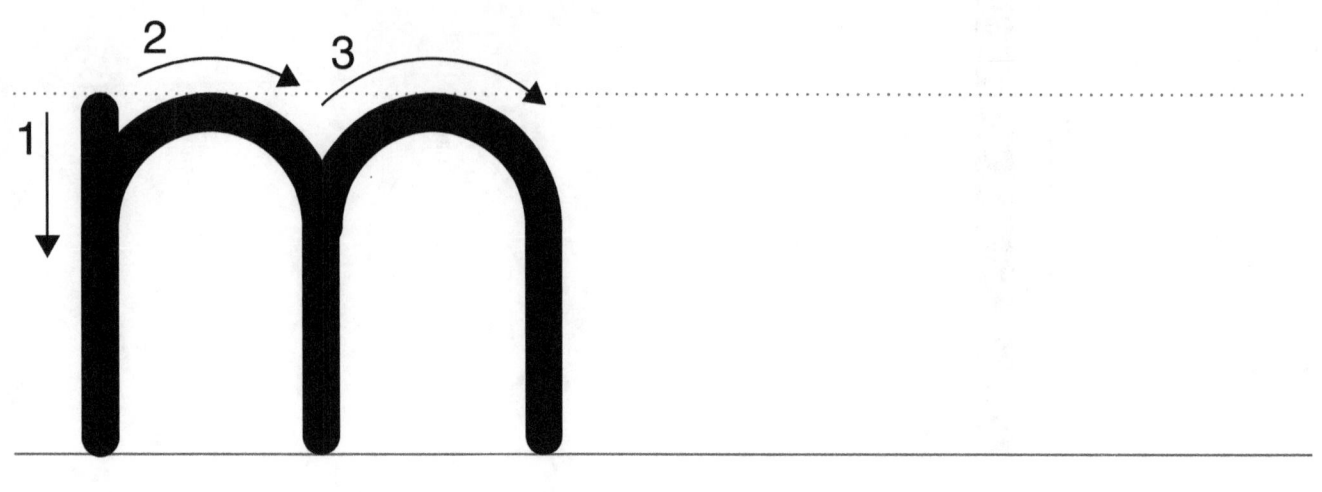

mmmmmmmmmmmm

mmmmmmmmmmmm

mmmmm

mmmmm

molly moose

makes music

nellie nag needs noodles

ozzie otter opens oysters

petie penguin

paints pictures

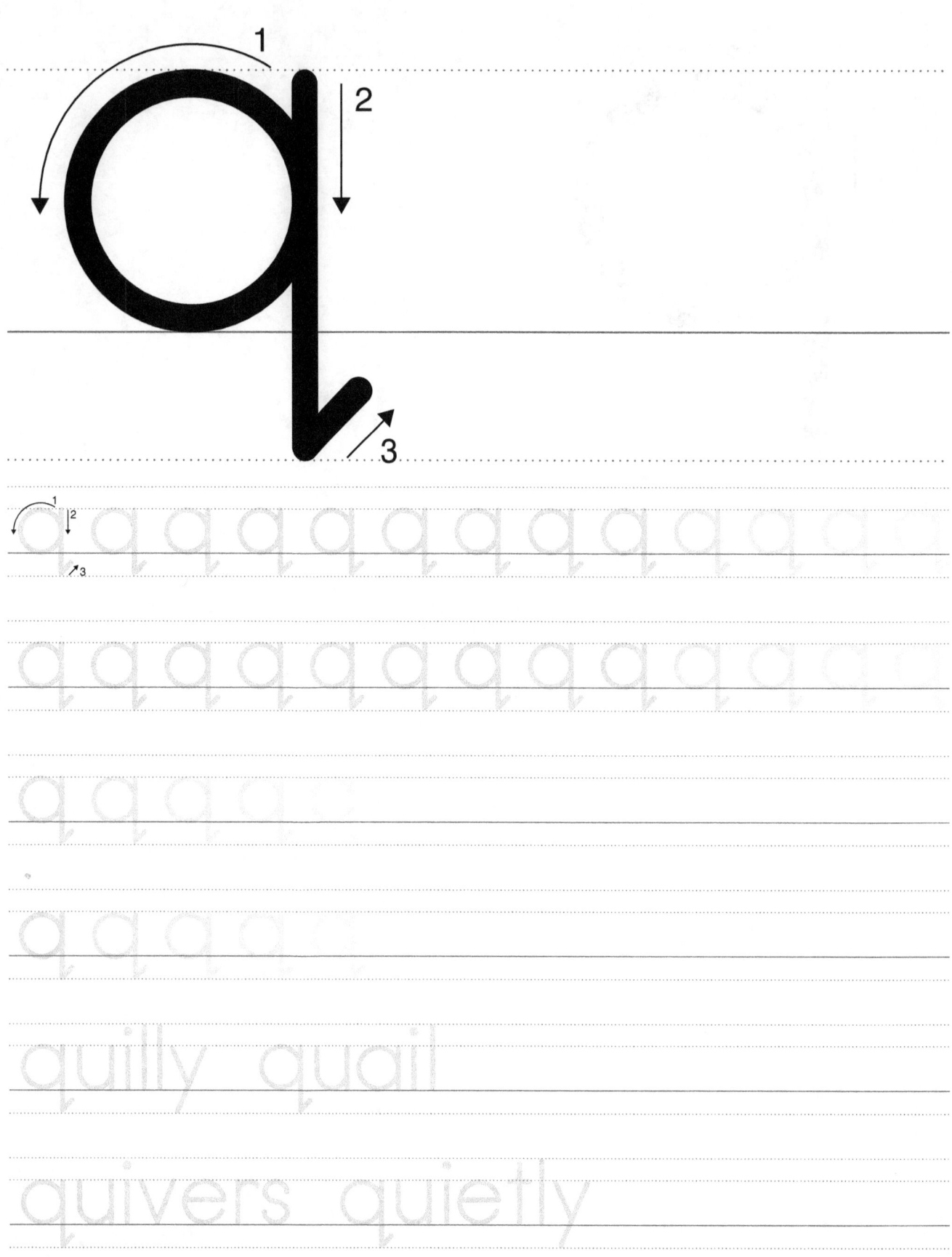

quilly quail

quivers quietly

rrrrrrrrrrrrrrrr
rrrrrrrrrrrrrrrr
rrrr
rrrr
rrrr

robbie rhino runs races

S S S S S S S S S S S S

S S S S S S S S S S S S

S S S S S

S S S S S

S S S S S

suzie seal sings songs

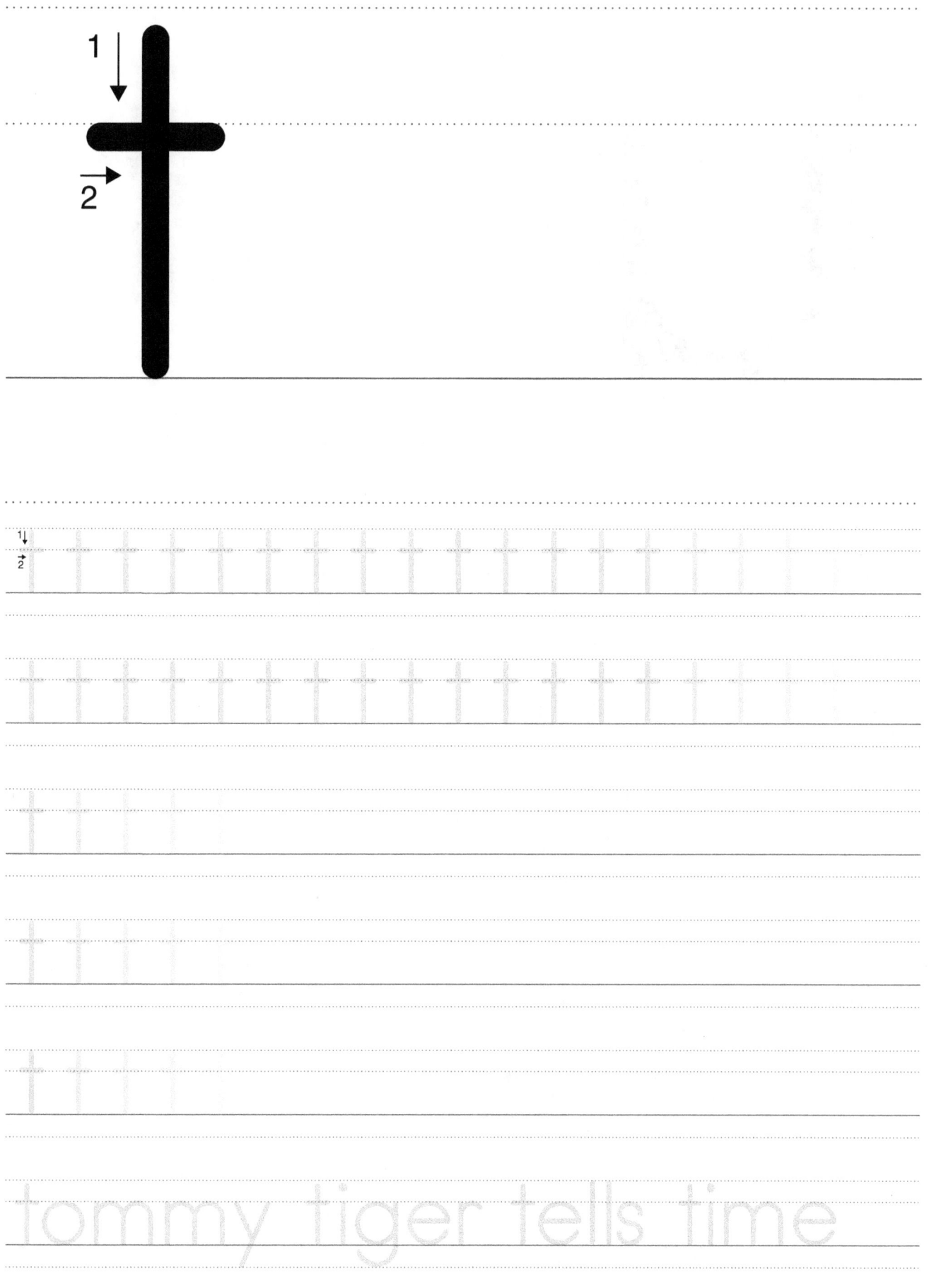

tommy tiger tells time

uuuuuuuuuuuuuu

uuuuuuuuuuuuuu

uuuuu

uuuuu

uncle unicorn

uses ukuleles

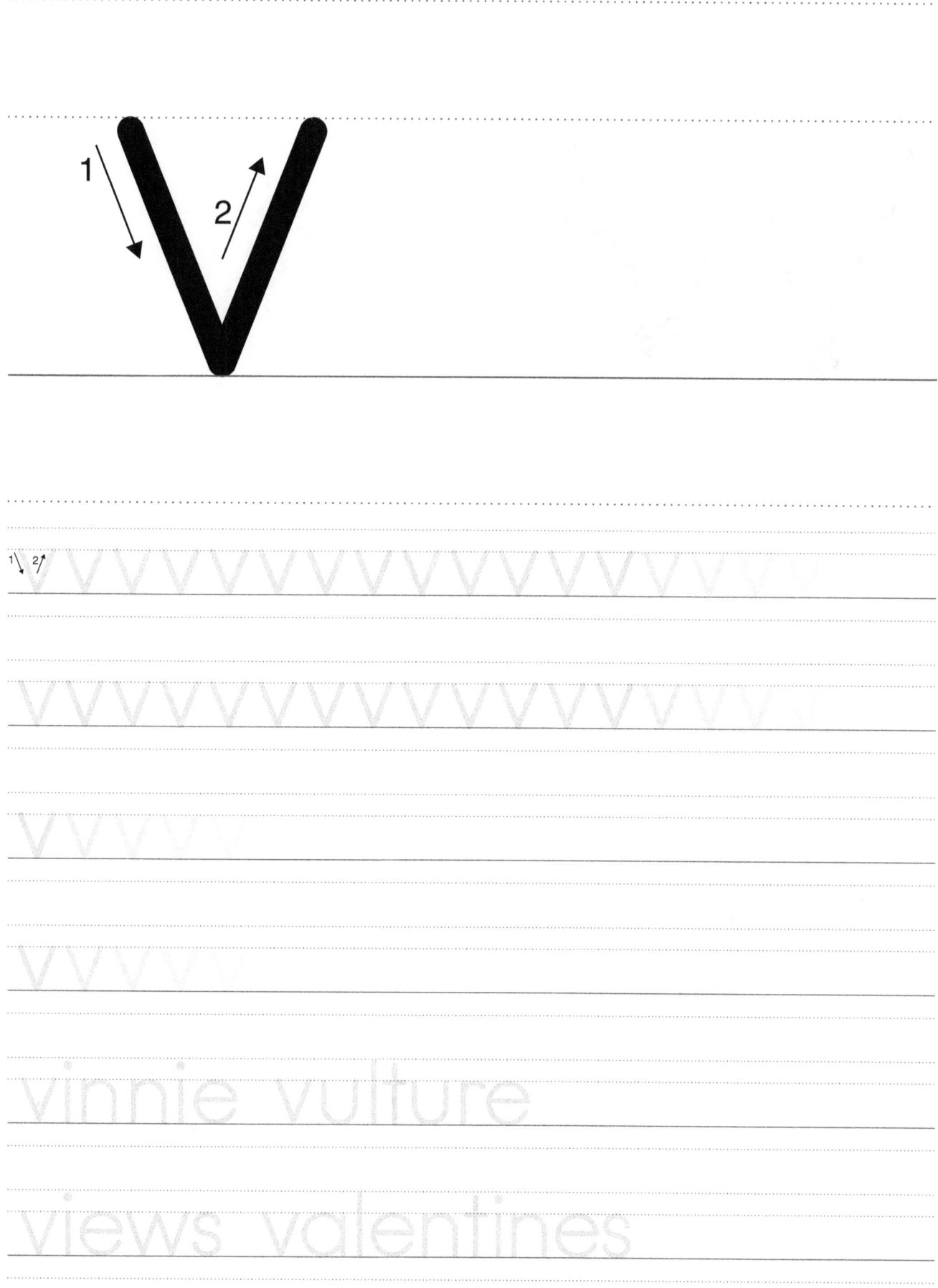

vinnie vulture

views valentines

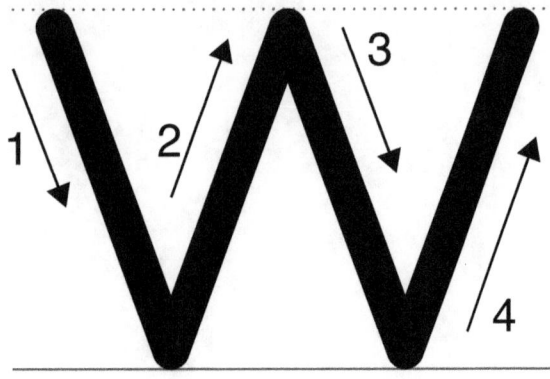

wally wolf washes wigs

x marks it wrong

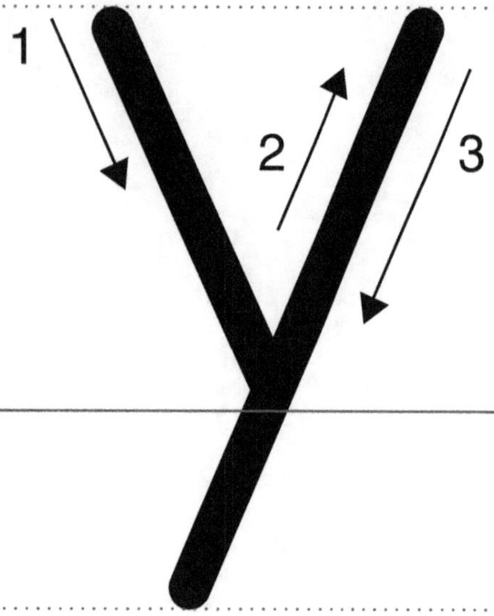

y

yyyyyyyyyyyyyyy

yyyyyyyyyyyyyy

yyy

yyyy

yyyy

yonita yak yodels yes

zeke zebra zings zithers